THE RV LIVING BLUEPRINT

A PRACTICAL, STEP BY STEP BEGINNERS GUIDE TO RV LIFE AND RV TRAVEL

JAMES WOLF

© Copyright 2021 - **All rights reserved.**

The content contained within this book may not be reproduced, duplicated or transmitted without direct written permission from the author or the publisher.

Under no circumstances will any blame or legal responsibility be held against the publisher, or author, for any damages, reparation, or monetary loss due to the information contained within this book, either directly or indirectly.

Legal Notice:

This book is copyright protected. It is only for personal use. You cannot amend, distribute, sell, use, quote or paraphrase any part, or the content within this book, without the consent of the author or publisher.

Disclaimer Notice:

Please note the information contained within this document is for educational and entertainment purposes only. All effort has been executed to present accurate, up to date, reliable, complete information. No warranties of any kind are declared or implied. Readers acknowledge that the author is not engaged in the rendering of legal, financial, medical or professional advice. The content within this book has been derived from various sources. Please consult a licensed professional before attempting any techniques outlined in this book.

By reading this document, the reader agrees that under no circumstances is the author responsible for any losses, direct or indirect, that are incurred as a result of the use of the information contained within this document, including, but not limited to, errors, omissions, or inaccuracies.

CONTENTS

An Introduction to RV Living   5

1. Is RV Living the Right Choice for You?   13
2. Finances   24
3. Choosing an RV   34
4. Essential Equipment for Your RV   56
5. Getting to Know Your RV   76
6. Power and Connectivity   90
7. Repairs and General Maintenance   106
8. Mailboxes and Healthcare   129
9. Camping and Boondocking   142
10. Safety and Well-being   152

Final Thoughts   165

SPECIAL BONUS

WANT THIS BONUS BOOK FOR FREE?

Get **FREE** unlimited access to it and all my new books by joining the fanbase!

AN INTRODUCTION TO RV LIVING

RV living is a lifestyle choice that's more itinerant and less stationary than standard 'sticks-and-bricks' style living.

It's a lifestyle choice for those who like to explore, who thrive on changes of scenery and taking in new experiences.

A choice for the explorers, the adventurers, the travelers, the wanderers, the innately curious, the naturally nomadic, and anyone else with a hardwired affinity for staying on the move.

RV living is a particular lifestyle choice made possible by living in an automobile or a trailer attached to another vehicle.

The unique rewards for those who choose this lifestyle are numerous and well worth the effort, it can be done on a small scale and within the limits of nearly any budget, but it is not for everyone. RV living has its advantages and disadvantages, like any other significant life choice.

It takes only the slightest hint of imagination to realize the incredible, life-changing and defining opportunities made possible by the sense of freedom and unending adventure afforded by a life on the open road.

RV Living is like nothing else in this world -- the opportunity to see some of the most extraordinary and splendorous sites this world has to offer, both well-known and obscure.

When you're RV living, there will be ample time and opportunity for all of it. It's little wonder why this pastime has seen such enormous popularity since its inception in the 1910s and continues to blossom more than a century later.

This enduring popularity is evident in the now-massive recreational vehicle industry, which continues to see record growth in the number of vehicles sold and the ever-increasing number of people interested in RV living.

This book is geared towards those considering making the change from a "bricks and sticks" based lifestyle to a life lived at least part-time in a recreational vehicle.

It will present an overview of things to consider before committing to this lifestyle, as well as the basics of what life in an RV entails.

This book is meant as an informative starting point on your journey, a first step in helping you get on the road and begin the adventure of a lifetime.

For those thinking about taking the plunge and researching this way of life, the first chapters of this book will detail some of the pros and cons and the questions one needs to ask themselves before they make this decision. In later chapters, this book will lay out some of the nittier, grittier details and the realities of RV Living.

These are some of the topics covered in this book:

Is RV Living Right for You?

As amazing, alluring, and unique as it is, RV living may not be for everyone.

If you are considering this lifestyle, then you clearly have the qualities that make an excellent RVer.

However, as with most substantial life changes, there is a range of practical matters to consider before committing, including the pros and cons of RV living

Finance

This chapter will go over the fundamentals regarding the financial elements of investing in and living life in a recreational vehicle.

First of all, you need to buy the RV itself, the cost of which can range from nothing to more than one million dollars. While most modern RV prices will land somewhere in the middle, your budget will play a role in narrowing down your choices and deciding which RV is suitable for you and your needs.

Of course, when it comes to the financial side of RV living, the initial purchase is only the beginning. The other expenses will also be discussed in more detail.

Choosing an RV

Shopping for any vehicle involves a series of crucial decisions. Choosing an RV is certainly no exception, as for many, this will also be a new home.

This chapter will detail the many different types of RVs there are to choose from and the advantages and disadvantages of each, along with what to look out for when shopping for an RV.

Equipment

In addition to the vehicle itself, there is other equipment essential to RV living which we will discuss in this chapter. In addition to the essentials, there are also several luxury items that some RV owners choose to buy.

Getting to Know Your RV

This chapter will introduce you to some of the basic features of your new home. While you may not need to know all of the nitty-gritty operational details of all of your vehicle's features when you first buy your RV, you will likely find these skills valuable at some point in the future.

This chapter will also give you some tips on where to store your things and set up your RV for maximum comfort.

Power and Connectivity

RV living does not mean a life without electricity! In this chapter, you will learn about the various ways you can stay powered while on the road. Also, in this day and age, staying connected is essential to most people.

This chapter will give you some great options for doing just that while living life on the road and the advantages and disadvantages of the different options you'll have for staying powered and connected.

Repairs and General Maintenance

Good upkeep is essential for keeping any home functional, but when your home is on wheels, it is even more critical.

This chapter will give you some tips on how to keep your RV running smoothly and efficiently.

In addition, this chapter will also address some of the more common issues that you could face when living on the road and how to deal with them.

Mailboxes, Healthcare, and the Realities of a Mobile Lifestyle

Of course, when your home is frequently moving, you will have to deal with some issues that homeowners who have fixed addresses do not.

In this chapter, you will learn about some of these issues and how to handle them.

Campsite Tricks and Boondocking

In this chapter, we will discuss some of the many different places you can stay in your RV.

These range from official campgrounds with all the amenities to "boondocking," which is essentially free camping on land where that is possible.

Safety and Wellbeing

RV living can be a fun and exciting experience. However, there are some potential dangers that you should be aware of before making the leap. Here we address some of those potential dangers and how to avoid or handle them.

RV living is unlike anything you've likely experienced before. The freeing feeling of your home being the open road is something which words cannot do justice. While you may not yet know what your own experience with RV living will bring or exactly what your future as an RVer will hold, this guide will give you a practical overview so you can start your journey with a prepared, knowledgeable and confident foot forward.

Simply picking up this guide shows that you are drawn to the unique, adventurous world that RV living represents and that you are ready to learn more about it. It does take a certain amount of passion and dedication to be a successful RVer, and by doing research like reading this guide, you are already off to a fantastic start.

Ready to take the next step and start delving into the ins and outs of RV living? If you are, then congratulations! The next step of your journey is just a page turn away.

1

IS RV LIVING THE RIGHT CHOICE FOR YOU?

When starting to learn about the RV lifestyle, the first question you might have is also the most basic: Just what is RV living, anyway?

RV living is a choice to live a life out on the open road instead of paying rent or a mortgage to stay in one place; you have an RV, your new home on wheels, which you can move from place to place whenever you need or want to.

This can be a temporary situation, perhaps while saving money for a house or moving seasonally to where the weather suits you best, or it can be a more permanent situation where you live in your RV full time.

Some people are forced into it due to losing their homes to foreclosure, but many just enjoy the freedom that comes with it. Are you fed up with the view? Just pack up and find a better one.

RV living is not one size fits all, and there are many different reasons people choose this way of life.

Whether or not RV living is right for you depends on your own personal situation and what you are looking for in life.

There are psychological implications that come with this lifestyle choice that you should be aware of before making your decision. These implications are different for each person, but one of the most common is a feeling of rootlessness and detachment from society at large. It can be challenging to maintain close relationships with friends and family who do not live this way.

The severity or even the existence of these implications varies widely, depending on your previous lifestyle and whether you choose to commit to part- or full-time.

However, whether you stay relatively stationary and keep much of your work and social life intact, or you plan to leave your former life behind and commit to a new, ever-changing adventure on the open road, there are some factors that anybody making the transition needs to consider.

For example:

- How much stuff do you have? It might be more than you realize.
- How much can you fit in your RV?
- How much can you afford to keep in storage?
- How much do you really need to take with you?
- What can you get along without or do without for a while?

These are questions that only you can answer. However, like so much about RV living—from the earliest stages of planning and research to the experience of life out on the open road—you may very well end up discovering a lot about what's really important to you.

Another factor to consider is whether you are ready to commit all of your time -- really your entire life -- to RV living. Perhaps it would be more practical or enjoyable to dedicate just part of each year to living in an RV while still keeping your home base intact.

You might also ask yourself if you would like to live in a self-contained motorhome or if a travel trailer attached to a vehicle would be more your style.

These are all questions that are not only important to ask before taking the plunge into the RV life but also may be an enjoyable part of planning this incredible journey you're only just beginning. It could also help to shed some light on your goals as a new RVer and what you would like to get out of the experience.

In addition to those personal considerations, there are some other factors that may be just as important.

The RV lifestyle has also changed in the last few decades and even over the last few years.

RV living used to be considered more of a hobby for those who had the time and the resources to give their lives to travel, and this was largely accurate at one time.

In this day and age, however, that is no longer necessarily the case.

RV living has become much more affordable over the years due to more efficient construction methods, the widening range of vehicles within the RV market, the growing number of RVs on the used market, and the increasing popularity of practices such as repurposing used buses, trucks and vans as motorhomes.

This means that there are more resources than ever available to aspiring RVers, and a growing understanding of this lifestyle amongst the general population.

For example, most cities and even some smaller towns now have RV parking areas where you can stay for a small fee. And the informational resources available when searching for paid parking or even free spots to park are exponentially more prevalent than they were in recent years.

However, as RV living booms in popularity, such parking areas and campsites in national and state parks can fill up fast, which is one example of how the RV boom in recent years has its disadvantages as well.

There is a substantial variety of things to consider if you plan to make this a full-time lifestyle choice.

In addition to the practical questions listed above, some of the more personal questions to ask yourself when trying to decide whether this lifestyle may be a good fit for you include:

- Do you like the outdoors? RV living provides an exceptional way to stay connected to the great outdoors for those who enjoy it.
- Are you a people person? While RV living is itinerant by its nature, you will still end up meeting and dealing with people from all walks of life throughout your journey, including fellow members of the RV community.
- Are you handy? The chances are high that you will need to put your mechanical skills to the test regardless of the rig you end up choosing, even if it is just for basic maintenance or light repairs. RV living presents a unique opportunity for self-sufficiency which may be hard work but is also rewarding like nothing else.

- Do you like to work on your own vehicle? RV living nearly always involves putting many miles on either your motorhome or the vehicle you're using to haul your trailer. Anybody who's inclined to enjoy doing their own vehicle repairs, maintenance, or upgrades will relish this aspect of RV living.
- Do you have a lot of stuff? Living in an RV means, by necessity, living a somewhat streamlined life by many modern standards. This is something to consider when weighing up the pros and cons of RV living.
- How much do you like to travel, and how far are you willing to go? RV living is definitely for travel lovers and those with an adventurous spirit who enjoy the journey as much as the destination.

Answers to some of these questions may come readily to you, even instantly. Others you may need to think about a bit longer, but they are all crucial to ask yourself. In fact, thinking about those questions which are not as easy to answer immediately may lead to some fresh, enlightening insights.

For example, you may realize that you do have a lot of stuff when you think about it, or that the number of possessions you have in your home may not seem like a lot but would still be too much to carry with you everywhere you travel. How much of your stuff do you think you'd be willing to do without, or at least to put into storage—which may lead to further questions.

Which possessions do you need to hold onto full time, or at all, and why?

RV living is not for everyone, but it just might be perfect for you.

It's a big world out there, and the unique life afforded by a recreational vehicle lends itself to giving you the time, the resources, and even the inclination and inertia it takes to explore as much of it as possible. You never know what amazing things you may experience if you open yourself up to new opportunities.

It takes a special kind of person to handle the day-to-day responsibilities of this unique way of life. If you're reading this book, you undoubtedly have at least some qualities that make an excellent RVer. It's not just about living in a vehicle. It is a state of mind.

What better place to start your new adventure than the centre of your new world, the RV itself. An RV is self-contained, providing everything you need for self-sufficient travel in one place, typically including a bathroom and a kitchen. There is no standard-sized RV, although there are basic categories and classes, which we will discuss in a bit.

At the very least, a standard RV has a bed, a bathroom, a kitchen area, and some storage space. It has also become ubiquitous for RVs to come with some basic entertainment functionality, including a TV and a DVD or Blu-ray player.

Some RVs have satellite dishes so that you can watch live TV whenever and wherever you want. However, it is increasingly common to use mobile internet access to stay connected to modern entertainment, communications, and even job options. Those options will be detailed more in the chapter on connectivity.

There is a wide range of vehicles encompassed in the RV category. Some are built for luxury, others for easy travel and living on the open road, and others constructed specially for wilderness excursions.

You can buy an RV from a dealership or directly from the manufacturer or buy a used RV from a private seller.

The price of an RV depends on the size, age, brand, and features. In the case of a used RV, age and condition will also play a significant role in cost while valid with any used vehicle. With a used RV, this is often more complex since considering the vehicular facets of the RV and the living space is essential.

After all, this is going to be a home. However, it is not a house, or an apartment, even if many find an RV to be a perfect place to live.

As myriad as the differences are between RV living and sticks-and-bricks living, one way to conceptualize the essence of what really separates these lifestyles is to think about what it actually means to be indoors versus outdoors.

When you are inside a building, like a house with a roof overhead, it obviously qualifies as being indoors. When you walk outside that house and are completely exposed to the elements, it's similarly apparent that you are outdoors.

But what about if you're camping, in a tent? A tent offers some level of protection from the elements, but the inside of a tent is still widely considered to be outdoors conceptually. A tent provides more protection from the weather and other outdoor hazards than, say, an umbrella, but it still could not compete with a permanent structure for shelter from the proverbial storm.

While an RV is a step up from the lightweight, attenuated material of most tents, the inside of a vehicle is still in many ways closer to that of a tent than a permanent structure.

While RV features vary widely, and some offer better structural protection from the elements than others, they do not provide nearly the same insulation or climate-minded design as a sticks-and-bricks building. Whether or not you'll consider your RV to be "indoors," you will be at the mercy of whatever is happening in the great outdoors in a way that the traditional idea of indoor life could hardly prepare you for.

Depending on when and where you are traveling with your RV and when and where you are staying, you are going to need to rely on your RV's heating and cooling system to at least some extent. Not only for your comfort but your mental and physical health as well.

Climate and weather-related concerns are amongst the reasons some choose only to dedicate part of the year to RV living, electing for the relative warmth and stability of a more traditional home during the months, which bring the least pleasant weather. Allowing more potentially budget-friendly RVs, such as pop-up campers, which are much more comfortable in temperate weather.

An RV, of course, can allow for the avoidance of many issues with seasonal weather thanks to its mobility. There are also other reasons that a contingent of RVers choose to stay in sticks-and-bricks for part of the year.

For one, the novelty of RV living, like anything else, can wear off eventually, and taking long breaks between RV sojourns can help keep things feeling fresh.

Dedicating part of the year to staying in sticks-and-bricks also allows you to keep connected to a community and a sense of permanence that some RVers do miss once they have been unmoored for a length of time.

Of course, keeping a sticks-and-bricks home part-time is not an option for everyone, and many choose to dedicate themselves full time to their RVs and the magical sense of adventure that only RV living can provide.

Most RV enthusiasts will tell you that one of the best feelings they get is when they are on the open road, in total control of their vehicle and their home.

For some, nothing less than full-time living out on the road is acceptable. For others, RV living is much more rewarding when practiced part-time. Finding the option which is right for you will go a long way towards ensuring you get the most out of your investment and in your commitment to RV living.

Chapter Summary

Welcome to the world of RV Living!

A brief summary of what we've discussed so far:

- RV Living is a lifestyle choice with something to offer for a wide range of people. It's like nothing else in the world, even if it's not for everyone.
- RV Living is quite different from the stationary, sticks-and-bricks lifestyle. There are some essential questions to ask yourself while planning your adventurous leap into this exciting new journey.
- Planning carefully and correctly preparing will go a long way towards ensuring that your RV Living experience is as rich and rewarding as it has the potential to be.

2

FINANCES

After making the decision to start RV living, you'll probably have plenty of questions. This chapter will go over some of the financial basics you'll need to get started.

The financial aspects of this decision likely loom large for anybody figuring out how to make this lifestyle work. For many, it may be more significant than any other facet of consideration.

This chapter will go over those aspects and take a look at some of the topics covered in other chapters from a finance-minded perspective.

First and foremost, your RV is going to be your new part-time or full-time home. It is likely to be a significant purchase, just like any new home, so it's essential to understand the financial aspect of this choice.

There is also the cost of maintaining your RV and keeping everything working the way that it should. RV living does have a reputation for being expensive, but you can avoid this with some forward-thinking and planning.

Your first step should be to find an RV that is right for you. Be sure to set aside time for test drives and for getting to know different models.

Before deciding whether to go the route of a new or pre-owned RV, you will need to consider the category of RV that would best suit your needs.

The major categories include Class A, B, or C motorhomes, a trailer that you would attach to another vehicle, or even a truck camper to convert the bed of a pickup truck to an RV.

For those with a family, or the need to carry a lot of cargo, a larger Class A or B motorhome might be best. Class A motorhomes are built from the ground up to be motorhomes exclusively and are considerably larger than Class B or C motorhomes.

These are ideal for larger families or those that require a lot of space. Class B motorhomes are built from the frame of a full-sized van, although the RV maker sometimes alters them to provide some more room for living.

If you are an outdoorsy type or just don't plan on spending a lot of time in your vehicle, a class B or a smaller Class C is more your speed. Class C motorhomes are built from the template of a van or truck, but they are generally much closer to a classic car or truck in style, making them easier to drive for anyone accustomed to driving a car or van. Many Class C RVs also offer more space or power than a Class B without the budget-stretching price point that many Class A RVs tend to carry.

There is also an array of non-motorized recreational vehicles on the market ready to hitch to a pickup truck or other vehicle appropriate for hauling such a load—from sizable "Fifth Wheel" trailers to lightweight teardrop campers that house a bed and little more.

Also in the RV category are vans, trucks, and buses, which have been converted into mobile living quarters. While we will discuss these categories in more detail later. Before going RV shopping, you will want to narrow down your choices according to needs and budget as much as you can while still keeping your options open.

The RV market is its own beast, which differs in many ways from the new or used car or truck market. There are several significant factors that you will want to take into consideration before setting out.

RV sizes range from smaller campers which can be towed by a half-ton pickup, to large motor homes capable of towing or hauling multiple vehicles themselves.

Non-motorized RVs are generally only an option if you have a suitable vehicle to tow them. Of course, there are exceptions, like the lightweight teardrop camper towable by a family SUV.

Generally, the larger the RV, the more they cost, but that is not always the case. In most cases, RVs are made for use on the road or in campgrounds. However, Off-road RVs are created to be taken off paved roads and into more rugged territory such as dirt roads or even mountainous areas. These will usually have special equipment and higher ground clearance to handle these situations.

Since you will be shopping for not only a vehicle but also a new home, you will want to cast as wide a net as possible and research all that you can. Search your local RV dealer and classified ads in local papers as well as trade shows. Manufacturer websites may offer a way to cut out the middleman, so to speak, and save on dealer costs while providing the ability to customize your new home if you have the budget and inclination.

Some RVs are built for extended stays in remote locations, while others are just designed for weekend getaways, so keep this in mind when looking over the available models. An RV suited for occasional or part-time use can be much kinder on your wallet than a vehicle designed to be a full-time home.

While motorhomes tend to soak up a lot of the glitz and publicity of the RV world, many RV owners elect for a non-motorized rig that you can hitch to a suitable vehicle for travel and unhitched for parking, camping, and storage situations.

Some RV owners will want to take smaller vehicles with them for more easy exploration of various destinations. Indeed, depending on your vehicle choice, you will have some options for this. Whether it's unhitching a trailer from your pickup or a bicycle or two in the back of your Class C RV. Hauling motorcycles and ATVs in a "toy hauler" meant for carrying such things—with built-in garage space and a ramp for easy loading and unloading—or even towing an SUV everywhere you go behind a sizeable motorized RV.

While the fuel costs for a non-motorized RV are non-existent and the maintenance costs are relatively low, these savings are offset to varying degrees with the costs of owning and maintaining a vehicle with the power and structural suitability needed to haul a large trailer.

Motorized RVs do have fuel and maintenance costs, of course.

However, these costs vary depending on the size of the rig you choose, the condition of the RV, and the type of engine. Many categories of motorhomes have diesel engine options, which have higher upfront costs but can save you money in the long term with better efficiency and less frequent maintenance.

While discussing the efficiency of different motorhome engines, it's difficult to ignore the elephant in the room of a rapidly changing automobile and energy industry.

Hybrid and electric cars, trucks, and SUVs have been taking those markets by storm with their excellent efficiency and reduced environmental impact. With all of that happening, it's understandable if you're wondering if there are any hybrid engine or even electric, motorized RVs on the market.

As of this writing, the answer is that we're going to have to wait a bit longer. While green technology is sure to catch up with fuel-hungry motorhomes sooner or later, for the time being, traditional gas or diesel engines are the only options in the motored RV market.

However, some smaller trailers could be affixed to and towed by a more powerful hybrid vehicle. While electric cars are not widely used for towing— it tends to drain their batteries faster and reduce their range between charges. That is changing as manufacturers like Ford and GMC are developing tow-capable electric trucks expected to hit the market in 2021 and 2022.

So, even if you want to minimize or avoid traditional fuel usage and carbon emissions with your RV Living, there are options out there. And with the imminent electric truck revolution, electric motorhomes cannot be far behind.

Other than the RV itself and any vehicles you may own and choose to tow, you may also want to consider your power requirements. Most campgrounds will have electrical hook-ups for you to plug into, which is by far the easiest option but not always possible or available. Onboard generators are a common feature in modern RVs, but they are not always the most economical option for all of your power needs.

Solar power is an increasingly popular option for RVers. Just like buying solar panels for a traditional home, investing in a solar panel kit will pay off in reduced energy costs. There are RV solar panel kits intended to provide electricity for all of your devices. Still, there are also less expensive solar kits intended to supply just some of your power and lighten the load on your generator and onboard battery. This has the effect of reducing your RVs fuel consumption, which will save you money almost immediately and lessen the wear and tear on your vehicle's electrical system, which will save you money in the long run.

We will discuss the solar panel option and other options for power on the road at greater length in the chapter about power and connectivity.

These requirements will also play a part in your financial life on the road. Things like banking and bill-paying will require connectivity to some extent, as will many major and minor purchases.

Many RVers will depend on connectivity for their work-life as well.

While RV living is popular with retirees, an increasing number of RVers have found that it is quite possible to embrace the lifestyle while still working part or full-time and, in many cases enjoying a thriving career.

An unlimited internet data plan for all of your devices is likelier to be more expensive than a wired home internet plan. But especially for those who plan to work remotely on the road, it is a necessary expense.

Some work from home, some take short-term jobs in resource towns for part of the week or month, and still more forgo a traditional career path in favor of something more free-form like music or writing, but one thing is certain: RV living allows for a great deal of flexibility.

The significant financial decisions involved with transitioning from bricks-and-sticks to RV living require a great deal of research, including the prices generally paid for the RV you would like to purchase, your financing options, and even if rental may be a better option currently.

As far as working on the road is concerned, that is another world of research you will want to undertake. There have never been more opportunities in the realms of online jobs or online remote work. However, if you plan to go that route while RV living, or if you're already working remotely, you should consider the costs of a reliable remote internet connection.

Most major carriers offer unlimited mobile data plans with a Wi-Fi hotspot you can keep in your RV, but options become pricier if you plan to travel outside of standard coverage areas. As an alternative to mobile internet, satellite internet hotspots provide coverage but at a higher price and slower speeds, precluding modern business practices such as video conferencing.

Internet options will also be detailed further in the power and connectivity chapter, but these issues are key to consider if you plan to take your work life on the road with you.

If being able to store additional possessions and valuables that you will not be able to take with you on the road is a necessity, storage space in an accessible location will be another regular expense. Many storage facilities do offer long-term discounts, however. It is worthwhile to look into renting a safety deposit box at a bank rather than a traditional storage locker for valuables.

Now that we've discussed some of the often less-than-thrilling financial aspects of RV Living, it's time to delve into the more exciting subject of finding the RV which is right for you.

Chapter Summary

Some of the key points to keep in mind when considering the finances involved with RV Living:

- The primary financial decision you will likely make as an RVer is which vehicle to purchase.
- There is a vast range of RVs available on the marketplace to suit nearly any price point. The financial considerations of your RV go beyond just the purchase price. Things like fuel efficiency,

maintenance costs, and resale value also need to be taken into consideration.
- Once you have your vehicle, the expenses you'll incur on the open road will vary depending on which options you choose for things like electricity and internet access.
- You'll also need to factor in fuel costs, food bills, and camping.
- There have never been more options for working remotely for those who prefer or need to work on the road. However, reliable internet access is imperative in this case and needs to be included in your budget as a necessary expense.

3

CHOOSING AN RV

There are several sources around for you to use in your search. The internet is, of course, full of information and resources, from classified ads to brand new RVs and everything in between. You can find RV groups on social media sites like Facebook or RV forums where people from all around the country get together and talk about their experiences and knowledge of RVs. These resources offer a wealth of information and are definitely worth spending some time on.

It is best to have a base of knowledge regarding different RV options before going online and researching what's available for sale or rent.

As mentioned in the previous chapter, there are numerous recreational vehicle categories, including motorized and non-motorized types. Of the motorized varieties of RV, there are several different classes, of which we'll get into more detail here.

CLASS A MOTORHOMES

Class A motorhomes are designed and built every step of the way to be comfortable homes on wheels. This starts with a chassis designed primarily to create a motorhome, while other classes are built on chassis designed for vans or trucks.

Class As do justice to the term 'motorhome.' Separate from the driver's compartment, these roomy, mobile houses boast spacious living quarters with bedrooms, kitchens, bathrooms, comfortable common areas, and generous amounts of storage space.

Class A motorhomes come in both diesel and gasoline-fuelled varieties. Diesel motorhomes are generally pricier as they have better range with more powerful engines that do not need as much service. As mentioned in the previous chapter, diesel is also usually cheaper and more efficient than gasoline. However, servicing a gas engine is much easier to do on your own, while diesel engine repairs or maintenance often require a specialist.

If you plan to possibly sell your RV at any point, diesel motorhomes frequently have a higher resale value than their gas-powered counterparts.

One significant consideration to note if you are looking into buying or renting a class A motorhome is its size. Compared to other types of RV, they are huge, both in height and length. This can be a problem when it comes to parking. You may find that many national parks and privately owned campgrounds have rules against allowing class A motorhomes to stay there, simply due to the amount of space they take up.

National parks and many campgrounds restrict RVs in terms of size rather than class, and Class A motorhomes vary in size. As part of your research, it is ideal to physically measure the length of any RV you're considering yourself if these restrictions are a concern—the maker's official specs may not be accurate.

Class A motorhomes are all commonly the most expensive type of RV.

The deluxe model of a Class A motorhome can easily boast a sticker price well into the six-figure range. When researching the newest and most highly publicized vehicles, sticker shock leads many people to choose to buy a used RV rather than a new one.

Of course, there are cheaper options available if such prices are not an option for you or if you would just prefer to spend less.

Class A motorhomes are too large to be kept at most storage locations, so you may end up bringing it everywhere you can more often than not. This means being comfortable driving a vehicle that can easily be twenty feet long, or more, than a full-sized sedan—not to mention much taller and broader. But if you have the space and the money, a Class A motorhome is one of the most comfortable types of RV on the road today, and RV manufacturers continue to go all out on the designs, features, and amenities offered in their newest models to stay competitive in a continuously growing market.

Class B and Class C RVs

These types of RV are similar in many ways to one another and different from the classes already discussed. Both are built upon different vehicle chassis rather than designed from the ground up as motorhomes

Class B motorhomes are built on a van chassis that may or may not have been altered (made slightly larger).

CLASS B RV

Despite their small size relative to Class A RVs, Class B motorhomes are usually spacious enough to include a bathroom and a kitchen along with the requisite living and sleeping area.

There is also a subcategory known as Class B+. Class B+ motorhomes are slightly larger than Class B's as their chassis has been adopted to create more room for living and sleeping.

However, all types of Class B motorhomes have the advantage of a smaller size for better efficiency and maneuverability and better accessibility to campsites and national parks.

Like their Class A cousins, Class B motorhomes are available in both gas and diesel engine varieties.

Because of their smaller size, Class B motorhomes are less expensive than Class A motorhomes but can still be pricier than other motorhome options.

A Class C RV is similar in many ways to a Class B RV. They are both smaller and less pricey than Class A RVs, and they both vary more widely in size and features.

A Class C RV can be built on either a truck or larger van chassis. This means that Class Cs are typically larger than Class Bs, which by definition are built on a van chassis and are often marketed as being compact.

The larger chassis of Class C RVs allows for more extensive floor plans and more amenities than can fit in a typical Class B. Many Class C RVs will also have a sleeper bunk extending over this front section—a sort of iconic look associated with RVing in general.

Because they retain the same maneuverability and drivability of a regular truck or van–and indeed often feel comparatively comfortable to drive for people accustomed to those vehicles. Class C RVs are popular choices for RV newbies and those who plan to drive their RV to the campsite rather than towing it. Class C motorhomes are also popular with the budget-minded who are interested in a reasonably spacious RV that feels a bit more like a traditional vehicle than a Class A.

CLASS C RV

Within the Class C motorhome family, although not quite as budget-friendly as traditional Class C's, is the subcategory known as the "Super C." These RVs are built on large truck chassis.

They have powerful diesel engines giving them an exceptional towing capacity and plenty of space. Super C motorhomes are often designed to appeal to a luxury market, so for those more concerned about comfort and amenities than budget, these RVs are worthy of serious consideration.

In addition to Class A, B, and C motorhomes and their subtypes, the category of motorized RV also includes other types of vehicles which have been converted for mobile living–namely buses, vans, and trucks.

Most of these retrofitted and altered vehicles are not available on the new market, so if you've decided that only a brand-new rig is going to be acceptable, then you can safely rule out this category.

These conversions are typically available for sale from some second-hand RV dealers or directly from the people who have performed the conversions from old decommissioned school buses, transit buses or sprinter vans, and even military vehicles.

However, a growing community has sprung up around the idea of finding older, sometimes non-functional large vehicles and converting them into mobile homes. This type of project can be an epic and ultimately gratifying undertaking for those with the time, know-how, and inclination to perform it themselves.

Of course, not every RVer interested in a fixer-upper type of project has quite that same level of ambition. Fortunately, the used RV market is full of budget-friendly options which may not currently be ready for the road but certainly are ready to be fixed up for a new lease on life.

The broad umbrella of the non-motorized RV category covers essentially any livable trailer which is meant to be towed—usually—by another vehicle.

TRUCK CAMPERS

An exception to this would be the truck camper, an RV that can mount right onto the bed of an appropriately sized pickup truck. These RVs are carried rather than towed, but this is an exception in the world of non-motorized RVs.

Truck campers have enjoyed enduring popularity over the last few decades as they use the existing structure of your truck to create a livable and highly portable RV with little to no increase to the truck's footprint. This allows you to take your RV with you anywhere your truck can go.

Truck campers are also generally easier to heat or cool than trailers. With most of these campers, you can park, maneuver, or fill up on gas just as easily as you could with your truck, and you can also store your RV when not in use even more easily than a smaller trailer. Some truck campers are collapsible when not in use for even more convenience. These "pop-up" configured campers come in both hard-side and canvas soft-side varieties. See the Pop-Up Campers section below for more details about this type of RV.

The convenient size of truck campers comes at the expense of roominess, however, and while bathrooms and cooking areas are offered with many truck campers, those amenities are far from standard. However, like every other variety of RV, there are upscale options available with all the bells and whistles, including campers with slide-outs for more space.

Long-bed pickups or dually trucks are an especially suitable type of truck to use with a truck camper, thanks to their roominess and high payload ratings for carrying an RV.

Truck campers come in a variety of different sizes, and of course, it's critical to choose a camper that fits the dimensions of your truck bed and will not exceed your vehicle's payload capacity. Remember that your RV will weigh more once it's furnished and loaded. Your truck's center of gravity will also need to be taken into account. That is something to research and discuss with your RV dealer.

TRAVEL TRAILERS

A popular alternative to the truck camper in the vast category of non-motorized RVs is the almost as vast subcategory of travel trailers.

Travel trailers are usually more affordable than truck campers and do not require a suitable truck bed for installation. These RVs are often a favored choice amongst new RVers as they are relatively light and easy to maneuver, and depending on their size and weight, they can be towed with a more lightweight vehicle such as a compact SUV.

A notable option in this category would be the compact and lightweight teardrop trailer. The smallest of these cozy trailers can be towed behind a standard sedan. These compact RVs have developed quite a following over the past decade—the Tearstock gathering held each year in Michigan is one of several annual conventions for teardrop camper enthusiasts.

FIFTH WHEEL TRAILERS

For RVers in need of ample space for living, sleeping, and storage, a Fifth Wheel trailer offers the luxurious roominess of a Class A motorhome without being motorized. Instead, Fifth Wheels are affixed to a capable vehicle using a gooseneck rig for towing. Unlike smaller RVs like truck campers or teardrop trailers, Fifth Wheels offer generous floor plans, typically with full bathrooms and kitchens.

Fifth Wheel trailers are popular with large families and groups traveling together thanks to their spacious floor plans and the ability to sleep up to twelve people. Fifth Wheels also frequently offer slide-outs to provide even more interior space. As you would expect, these RVs require a formidable vehicle to tow them—at least a half-ton pickup truck. However, a three-quarter-ton or larger truck with a long bed is ideal for safety and maneuvering while towing one of these "mansions on wheels."

TOY HAULERS

For RVers who require beaucoups of space for their smaller vehicles such as motorbikes, all-terrain vehicles, and snowmobiles, toy haulers are a perfect solution. Toy haulers look like a large trailer such as a Fifth Wheel from the outside, but they are designed specifically for storing, hauling, and easy loading and off-loading of various small (well, smaller) vehicles with a rear ramp. Some toy haulers come with combined living and vehicle storage areas, and some larger toy haulers have their own living areas with a separate rear "garage" for vehicles.

POP-UP CAMPERS

Pop-up campers combine affordability for the budget-conscious RVer with a lighter weight that can be towed with a broader range of vehicles. These campers are perfect for shorter camping trips and overnight adventures in agreeable temperatures, but they offer little in the way of permanent living or storage space. Bathrooms and kitchens are a rarity in this category and do not stand up well to extended periods of inclement weather.

Pop-up campers are available in a variety of sizes and configurations, including pop-up versions of truck campers. Easy to collapse and store, pop-up campers are popular with those who RV only on occasion or are willing to sacrifice comfort and amenities for exceptional affordability.

RV SHOPPING - WHAT TO KNOW AND WHAT TO LOOK OUT FOR

Whether you are visiting your local RV dealership or scouring the local classifieds for an RV, you will need to be prepared with a list of questions to ask the seller. It would help if you also had a basic understanding of RV jargon so that you can easily communicate with your dealer and avoid ending up with a less than ideal investment for your money.

If you're buying a used RV from either a dealer or a private seller, it's best to get a professional inspection from a third-party mechanic, ideally, one you know and trust.

However, you can get a preliminary picture of the vehicle's condition and help make your inspection more efficient by asking a few questions of a private seller before proceeding with further research.

Are there any leaks?

Any leak will necessitate a potentially costly repair.

What is the condition of the tires?

If the tires' treads have worn down, or if they've aged to the point their structure has started to break down, they will need to be replaced before the RV is safe for travel.

Is there any rust on the undercarriage or body?

Rust is not uncommon in used RVs, and surface-level rust can be cleaned relatively easily. However, once rust starts to get deeper it can spread fast and start to comprise the vehicle's structure.

How old is the RV?

The age of a used RV will give you a great starting point for approaching further research of that vehicle and the scale of potential quirks and issues to be wary of. It will also give you a good starting point for researching that particular vehicle. Often, specific model years of a particular model RV will have quirks or common issues that you can learn about by a quick online search.

For example, searching for that model in a search engine can bring up results from an RVing forum like RV.net or a consumer review site like RVInsider.com where you may find common complaints about that model like a cramped bathroom layout or an underpowered electrical system. Some issues could be a matter of opinion, such as the design of a floor plan, and some could be more serious, like mechanical issues.

However, this research will only form a part of your decision-making process. The questions you ask your seller, your inspections, and in some cases, the assessment performed by your mechanic are of the utmost importance.

Is there any damage to the interior?

The RV's age is also crucial for research to see if there are common problems for that model year and to compare prices.

Does it have a generator?

A functional generator will save you the cost of having to buy a new one for your RV's electricity—unless you plan to upgrade the generator or overhaul the electrical system.

Does it have air conditioning?

Even moderately hot weather can mean intense discomfort inside a vehicle. Air conditioning is a must for full-time RV Living, and having to install a cooling system will bring substantial hassle and expense. If the RV does have air conditioning, ask if the air conditioner has had any issues leaking condensation inside the RV. A leak may mean that the unit needs cleaning, but failing that can also indicate the bolts mounting the unit to the vehicle need tightening or the gasket needs to be replaced. If the unit blows hot air or no air at all, this could also be a cleaning issue or Point to a more significant electrical problem.

Are there any modifications or aftermarket additions?

Some modifications—such as superchargers, replacement exhaust systems, or suspension upgrades–will void an RV's warranty if it was still in effect. They may also make the RV less safe, which is a good reason to research any mods of the vehicle itself. On the other hand, some modifications and additions may add to the vehicle's comfort, safety, and livability. Especially in an RV, where things like LED lighting and new plumbing fixtures can make a huge difference.

Does it come with an owner's manual?

You'll want an owner's manual for your RV, of course. If it doesn't come with one you may be able to find a PDF version online. Otherwise, finding one could be a hassle.

Does it have a title?

Motorhomes, trailers, and campers all need titles of ownership, with the exception of some lighter pop-ups in some localities. If you're buying used, it's something you'll want to secure by the time the sale is finalized.

How much does it weigh?

For trailers especially, you'll need to know if the max weight, or gross vehicle weight rating, is within your towing capacity.

Is it street legal?

Some older or heavily modified vehicles may not be ready to hit the road without some work or alterations. You don't want to wait until after you've made your purchase to find this out.

Many of these questions will be relevant to any RV buyer, while some will only be relevant to buyers in certain situations. Additionally, there are some things you will still want to examine yourself. For example, if the RV seller claims there's no interior damage, it is always best to examine the interior and exterior of the vehicle before purchase.

The point of these questions is not only for the information to use in your decision-making but also to make sure you and the seller are on the same page and that no false advertising is taking place.

And of course, showing that you're informed right off the bat is always a good message to send any seller.

It is important to remember that there is no such thing as a standard RV. Each one is different and will have its own set of strengths and weaknesses. It is up to you to decide what kinds of features are most important to you and which you are willing to do without.

Finally, you will need to keep an eye out for red flags when buying an RV from any source.

These red flags include:

- No title or a temporary registration (in the case of a private seller).
- The seller is vague about the RV's history.
- The RV is priced far below what it should be.
- The seller claims the RV is worth much more than it really is.
- The RV has been sitting in one place for an extended length of time (indicating that the owner doesn't use it).
- The seller seems hesitant to let you examine the vehicle.
- In the case of a used RV, the seller does not want the vehicle inspected by a mechanic.
- The RV has been recently painted (possibly to cover up any damage).
- The seller is asking for an unusually low price.
- The RV is in excellent condition, but the price is far above average.
- The seller claims the RV is worth much less than it really is.

Researching the make, model, and model year of the RV will come into play for some of these red flags, namely those that deal with the vehicle's value.

For used vehicles of any kind, getting a Vehicle History Report will be a crucial part of the research process.

A VHR can tell you the complete history of a vehicle, including accidents, damage, and any other information that may be pertinent to your decision.

These reports are easily obtained through several different private companies, with Autocheck and Carfax being among the most popular.

Chapter Summary

The basics to remember when choosing the right rig for you include:

- The major categories of RV include both motorized and non-motorized options, the latter usually requiring a suitable vehicle for hauling.
- The main classes of motorhomes include classes A, B, and C. Class A motorhomes are generally the largest. Class B and C motorhomes vary in size and are built on truck or van chassis. Some motorhomes on the used market have been converted from old trucks or buses.
- Non-motorized RVs include travel trailers of all sizes, from massive Fifth Wheel vehicles to lightweight teardrop campers. Truck campers are a popular option to convert a pick-up truck into an RV rig without the necessity for towing.

- Know which questions to ask before you start RV shopping, and know the things to look out for.

4

ESSENTIAL EQUIPMENT FOR YOUR RV

One way that purchasing an RV is different from buying almost any other type of vehicle is that it is doubtful that your new rig will come with everything needed for you to set out on your journey.

This is especially true for new RVs, which are sold "bare bones" to keep the initial price as low as possible.

While you can undoubtedly add most of these things as options when you buy a new RV, there are some things that you will need to have either before your RV arrives or immediately after. In this chapter, we'll discuss some of these items by category.

Essential RV Plumbing Equipment

Sewer Hose and Connection:

When your vehicle is going to carry everything you need for daily life, your plumbing system will be of the utmost importance. You will need to ensure you have the proper equipment for it or be functional before setting out.

A sewer hose is needed for the necessary task of draining your RV's sewage tank. It has a special fitting on each end, one of which will screw into the outlet on the back of your RV. The other will screw into the outlet at designated dumping stations designed for disposing of RV sewage.

These hoses are available in different lengths, with the longest reaching up to 100 feet.

Some RVs may come with a sewer hose and even a connector, but you cannot rely on either of these pieces of essential equipment to be part of your vehicle package.

Since you'll want your sewage hose to be of sufficient length for emptying at different locations, it's a good idea to opt for a hose of at least 15 feet in length, if not longer.

Thicker material is undoubtedly preferable for this hose, with quality sewer hoses boasting a thickness of 23 millimeters or more. Some additional features you may want to opt for in a sewer hose, depending on budget, are easy collapsibility and storage, a clear viewing window to ensure proper drainage, and fittings that are already attached.

Some sewer hoses are easily upgraded, with extensions already available. This may be something to consider if you are building a budget rig with an eye towards expansion in the future.

An RV sewer connection is a specialized fitting that screws into the outlet on the back of your RV and then connects to the sewer hose.

If you have a traditional flush toilet in your RV, you will also need a special holding tank for sewage known as a "black tank."

There are also liquid-only holding tanks known as "gray tanks." Gray tanks hold liquid only from sinks and showers. Some RVs have both gray and black tanks. We will discuss these tanks and RV plumbing in general in further detail in the following chapter on Getting to Know Your RV.

Sewer Hose Reel and Storage

If you want a convenient storage solution for your sewer hose that will also add to its ease of use, you may want to get a sewer hose reel. This will allow you to neatly store the sewer hose on the reel so that it doesn't take up too much space when not in use.

Water Hose and Water Filter

An RV fresh water hose is used for filling your fresh water tank. It screws into the RV's fresh water inlet. Some people prefer to use a water filter on their fresh water hose to keep it, and consequently, your fresh water supply, free of sediment and other debris.

Water Pressure Regulator

A water pressure regulator is a device that screws onto your RV's fresh water hose and reduces the pressure coming from the external water supply. This is necessary for filling your fresh water tank, as the high pressure of certain water hookups can damage your RV's pipes and pump. A water pressure regulator will also help to conserve water, as lower pressure will require you to manually turn on the faucet rather than having it come out at full force.

Your water pressure regulator is one piece of essential RV equipment you will want to avoid skimping too much on the price. A regulator that simply clips the water pressure at the same rate will often prove insufficient depending on your water hookup.

An adjustable water pressure regulator is a far better option.

Some essential accessories you'll want to pick up for your RV's water and sewage operation and maintenance include:

- A supply of holding tank treatment to help deodorize your RV's holding tank and prevent clogging issues.
- Some durable, disposable gloves, naturally.

Traditional RV holding tank treatment is made with formaldehyde, and these chemical-based products cover up odors and help break down solids and prevent clogs to some extent.

There are formaldehyde-free chemical holding tank treatments as well. For those who prefer all-natural cleaning products, bacteria-based holding tank treatments are relatively new in the RV world and use microbes to eliminate waste and odors organically.

However, bacteria-based holding tank treatments may have to be applied more often than chemical products.

Essential RV Electrical Equipment

Surge Protector or Electrical Management System

An RV surge protector is an essential piece of equipment for protecting your recreational vehicle's electrical system from power spikes.

A power spike can be caused by anything from a lightning strike to a short in a power line, and it can have a seriously detrimental effect on your RV's electrical system.

A power spike can not only damage your RV's electrical system, but it can also pose a fire hazard. A good RV surge protector will help to protect your RV's wiring and appliances from these surges.

Offering further protection for your vehicle's electronics than a surge protector would be an Electrical Management System or EMS.

An EMS is a more advanced version of a surge protector, and it will monitor your RV's electrical system for any abnormalities. If an EMS does detect an issue, it will automatically shut off the power to your RV before any damage can be done. An EMS is an excellent investment if you want to ensure the safety of your RV's electrical system.

You'll find that many RV parks offer free electricity, but some charge a small fee. If you are connected to one of these exterior power sources, protection in the form of a good surge protector or an EMS is a must-have.

Generator

If your RV does not come with its own generator or you find that you need more power than what is available from your RV's onboard generator, you may want to consider purchasing a stand-alone generator.

A generator can be run on gasoline, diesel, liquid propane, or a combination of gas and propane. The type of fuel a generator uses is one of the determining factors of the operating cost. Other factors will include the generator's capacity and efficiency.

You will also need to make sure that your RV is equipped with the proper connections for the type of generator you have purchased. Some generators are intended as permanent fixtures in an RV, and others are more portable by design. We will dive further into different types of generators and their pluses and misuses in the power and connectivity chapter.

ESSENTIAL KITCHEN ACCESSORIES FOR YOUR RV

Your RV may be equipped with a kitchen, but that doesn't mean you won't need any other equipment. You will probably find that you need more than a few things to help make your time in the kitchen a little easier.

Here are some essential kitchen accessories that you will want to have in your RV:

Cutting Board

It seems obvious, but you will need a cutting board to chop and prepare your food on, just like in any kitchen.

Popular choices are plastic, wood, or bamboo cutting boards.

Collapsible Food Prep and Storage Containers

These are great for organizing and storing food. Square or rectangular is the most efficient shape. These containers can also be stacked, making the best use of space in your RV.

You can also collapse them to about a third of their size, making them easy to store when you aren't using them. You will find that these containers are great for leftovers and packed lunches, as well.

Stacking Bowls

When space is at a premium as it's likely to be in your RV's kitchen, stackable bowls for serving are an investment that will continue to pay off in terms of convenience and saved space.

Durable Cookware

You will want to make sure that you have a good set of cookware in your RV. At least one set of the standard pots and pans you would need for meal prep is a good start. This is another set of essential items that it's worth investing a few extra dollars in to ensure your cookware will ensure the experience of heavy use on the road.

Cast iron equipment, although heavy, is also great for longevity and versatility.

Coolers and Cooler Accessories

A cooler is a fantastic, and for many RVers essential, thing to have if you plan on spending a lot of time outdoors or traveling.

Of course, coolers serve the important function of keeping food and drinks cold while you are traveling. However, this overall functionality can come in handy in a variety of ways while RV Living.

For example, you can use a cooler to keep perishables fresh after your grocery store runs. If you are boondocking or dry camping, a cooler will let you keep food from spoiling for extended periods of time.

Coolers come in all shapes and sizes, but RV Living calls for a cooler that will last longer and can handle more rugged conditions.

Just like certain types of RVs, coolers come in soft-side and hard-side varieties.

Soft-Sided coolers are great for RV Living, as they are made to withstand a lot of wear and tear. They are also lightweight and packable, so you won't have to worry about them taking up too much room in your RV.

Hard-sided coolers are more durable than soft-sided coolers, making them ideal for activities like fishing, boating, or camping when you'll need a cooler which will be rugged enough to withstand the outdoors in different kinds of weather and travel conditions. Also, they can usually hold a lot more food and drinks than soft-sided varieties, so they are great for long trips.

While hard-sided coolers are more durable than soft-sided coolers, they are also much heavier and take up more valuable real estate. You will want to make sure that you have enough room in your RV to store these types of coolers.

If you're planning to use your cooler, which is a good idea for longer camping trips and outdoor journeys, there are some must-have accessories to maximize its utility.

These include a cooler-top cutting board to provide a convenient food prep surface wherever you take your cooler. Also, a cooler-mounted bottle opener so you'll never find yourself camping or boondocking in the middle of the wilderness without a way to open your bottles.

While cutting boards and bottle openers add priceless convenience and utility to your cooler, the best way to enhance the usefulness of any cooler is cooler packs. These inexpensive, reusable packs can be put in with your food and drinks to keep everything cool for longer than would be possible with just ice or with your cooler's insulation abilities alone.

These packs stay in your RV's freezer, and the small amount of extra power it takes to keep them frozen will be worthwhile for those who plan to picnic and enjoy other outdoor activities that call for a cooler often.

ESSENTIAL RV EQUIPMENT FOR COMFORT

While your RV may have come equipped with a mattress or mattresses already, there are some other things you may want to look into getting if you're going to make your RV experience as comfortable as possible.

Mattresses and Mattress Toppers

One way to enhance the standard mattresses that come with your RV without investing in an entirely new mattress is a memory foam mattress topper.

These mattress toppers are made from viscoelastic—aka slow-rebound—memory foam that will mold perfectly to your body. They will give you the comfort and support that you need for a good night's sleep.

However, many RVers prefer to invest in an entirely new mattress, which will likely go further than a foam topper alone to ensure as much comfort as possible and a good night's sleep while on the road.

While there are naturally many types of mattresses available, memory foam mattresses are one of the most popular for the aforementioned comfort and support which the material provides, as well as their shock-absorbing qualities.

However, foam mattresses can take a while to break in compared to spring mattresses, and depending on how the foam was manufactured; there may be an "off-gassing" period of a day or two in which the mattress emits a chemical odor if it's brand new.

For RVers who may want to go on camping trips away from their vehicle or keep an extra bed around in case it's needed, an air mattress might prove helpful.

Air mattresses work the same in RVs as they do in traditional indoor living: great for a night or two, like if you're hosting a guest or going on a camping trip. However, these inexpensive beds are not made for long-term use and can lead to some very interesting mornings where you wake up lying on the floor of your RV.

Regardless of which type of mattress you opt for, make sure you get the right-sized mattresses for your RV (some vehicles only fit special RV-specific mattress sizes in their beds). Don't forget to plan for storage or disposal of any RV mattresses you'll be replacing.

Pillows and Other Bedding for your RV

Even setting aside potential concerns about aesthetics, comfort, or durability, any bedding that may come with your RV will not be enough for daily life on the road. You will need to supplement whatever bedding you do have with a few more pillows and blankets. Fleece blankets are a popular choice for RVs as they are lightweight yet still warm. Especially important if you live in a cold climate or plan on spending much time outdoors in your RV.

A good quilt or comforter is something else worth having in your RV's bedding inventory. If you will be traveling in colder regions or even places where it gets cold at night, a good comforter will go a long way towards making up for your RV's lack of bricks and sticks-like insulation.

Pillows are the last important piece of the RV bedding puzzle. A wide range of pillows is available for RVs, from standard cotton or down pillows to more specialized memory foam pillows.

Memory foam pillows tend to be a bit pricier but carry with them the same advantages as memory foam mattresses.

ESSENTIAL MISCELLANEOUS TOOLS AND GADGETS FOR YOUR RV

The following are some odds and ends which may not fit perfectly into other categories but remain indispensable for RV Living.

RV-Specific GPS

GPS units have come a long way since their inception. They are now small enough to fit in the palm of your hand, and there are even models designed specifically for RVs. These RV-specific GPS units have features like lane assistance to help you stay on route, as well as campground information. They can be a great asset if you are new to RV Living and don't want to get lost or waste time driving around looking for a place to stay. The GPS capabilities of modern smartphones are decently suited for basic RV navigation, but an RV-specific unit will frequently come in handy.

Tire Pressure Mounting System

If you are going to be towing your RV, a tire pressure mounting system is a must. These systems automatically keep track of your tire pressure and inform you when one of your tires starts losing air.

This can help you avoid having a flat tire and be an early warning system for a faulty tire, saving you time, money, and hassle.

Spare Tires

Even with storage space at a premium and any extra weight making your rig more fuel-thirsty, you don't want to get caught in the middle of nowhere with a flat and no way to switch it out.

Some new RVs come with spare tires, but many don't—especially more petite models. A single unmounted spare tire takes up quite a bit of room, but you'll be glad it's there if one of your tires is breached by some sharp gravel or gives out in the summer heat.

Leveling Blocks

If you are going to be staying in campgrounds that don't have full hookups, you will need some way of leveling your RV.

You can do this with basic bricks or blocks, but specialized products are designed precisely for this purpose.

Leveling blocks, also known as utility blocks or jack pads, are square blocks made specifically to level an RV. You can stack them to adjust the level of your vehicle. These blocks are especially beneficial if you need to raise one side of your RV higher than the other.

Toolbox and Set of Tools

The toolbox and set of tools you choose to bring with you will depend on your skill level and how much you think you are going to need them. If you are a beginner at RV Living, you might want to consider a basic toolset with everything you could possibly need to fix minor problems. If you have more experience, you might want to choose a more specialized toolbox. Either way, you are going to need the following tools:

- Screwdriver bits (various sizes in flat and Phillips Head formats)
- Cordless Driver / Drill
- Wrenches and socket wrenches (multiple sizes)
- A Multitool
- A Multimeter
- Hammer
- Pliers
- Towels and Rags
- Electrical tape and Duck Tape

Spare Parts

No matter how hard you try, something is bound to break or wear out while you are out on the road. It is a good idea to keep a few extra parts on hand for your RV just in case something breaks. These parts can be anything from light bulbs to fuses to hoses. You should also bring along the tools necessary to change them.

Portable Air Compressor and Accessories

It's always a good idea to bring along a portable air compressor.

These compressors are pretty easy to use and can save you a lot of time and effort, and they are especially useful if you find yourself in an area without access to air. You can simply fill up your RV's tires and be on your way. They also come in very handy for filling up air mattresses, sports equipment, and even pool toys.

ESSENTIAL RV ADD-ONS

While these additional options for your RV are not universally essential, they are still extremely popular and considered crucial by a substantial portion of the RVing population.

Many of these items are designed to make your RV easier to drive or more comfortable for you and your passengers.

Awning

An awning is a great way to extend your living space outdoors. They are easy to set up and provide a nice shaded area to sit, relax, do some grilling, or just take in some fresh air.

Most awnings can be retracted when the sun goes down or if it starts to rain. They are available in manual and electric models.

Roof Rack

If you like to go mountain biking, surfing, or kayaking then a roof rack is a great way to transport your gear. There are many different types of racks for transporting different types of equipment. Roof racks are also a classic way to squeeze the most out of the storage space options your RV will provide.

Tow Hitch

If you want to tow a vehicle behind your RV, you'll need a tow hitch. You can either have one professionally installed or perform the installation yourself. The type of tow hitch you choose will rely on what you are planning to tow behind your RV.

Of course, if you are choosing any sort of trailer as an RV, your towing equipment will be an absolutely essential part of your rig and something to research and consider as carefully as the vehicle itself.

Bike Rack

Similar to a roof rack, a bike is another way to take a bicycle or two with you while RV Living without using up precious space inside of your vehicle. A bike rack can be installed on the back of your RV and serve as an alternative to a roof rack or as additional space if your roof rack is already full of other gear.

RV Window Treatments

The blinds or curtains included with your RV may be sufficient, but If you want to block out the sun, privacy is a concern, or you just want to make your RV more like home, then you may want to consider installing additional window treatments. There are many different types of window treatments that can be installed in RVs.

RV blinds are a good option if you want to control light and heat. These are often used in conjunction with solar shades for more granular control over temperature and shade. As another option, RV shutters also offer significant protection from and control over the natural lighting and temperature of your RV while also adding a touch of personal style to your vehicle.

Chapter Summary

The essential equipment you'll want to pick up for your RV includes:

- Plumbing gear like a sewer hose and connectors, a

fresh water hose, water filters, a water pressure regulator, and durable gloves for emptying your tanks.
- Electrical equipment including a suitable surge protector or Electrical Management System and a generator if there's not one already onboard your vehicle.
- Kitchen essentials: cutlery, cutting boards, stacking bowls, collapsible food storage, durable cookware, bottle openers, and an appropriate cooler.
- Bedding that's properly sized to fit your RV's beds, including mattresses, pillows, linens, and comforters. Different types of mattresses have their pros and cons, but foam mattresses are by far the most popular for modern RVers.
- All the necessary tools and gadgets which your RV may not already have, including an RV-specific GPS, spare tires, a tire mounting system, leveling blocks, a portable air compressor, and a toolkit.
- RV add-ons essential for your experience, such as awnings, bike racks, window treatments, a roof rack, and a tow hitch.

5

GETTING TO KNOW YOUR RV

When you familiarize yourself with your new RV, you will be familiarizing yourself with your new home. However, your RV is unlike any home you'll experience in bricks-and-sticks life. You will need to get to know your new surroundings.

This chapter will give you a rundown of a typical RV and all its bells and whistles.

RV Sleeping Arrangements

RV living is unique in that it allows its users to travel and sleep in the same vehicle. Beds are as varied as the RVs that contain them, ranging from simple sofa beds to overhead bunks to extravagant master suite centerpieces. In this section, we'll take a look at some of the more common RV bed styles...

Traditional Beds

While smaller vehicles will only have space for beds that serve a double purpose, like the types listed below, larger RVs such as Class A motorhomes or Fifth Wheel trailers will usually have a "traditional" bed included in the floor plan. That is a bed that is just a bed and isn't designed to be a sofa or a dining table during the day.

As you might imagine, these beds are typically more comfortable than a bed that becomes another piece of furniture or folds into the wall. Some more sizable RVs may have more than one of these beds, and many have spacious master bedrooms with the equivalent of a king-sized bed.

The reason for the word "equivalent" here is that RV bed sizes are highly varied and often—although not always—differ from standard bed sizes. This is why it's crucial to know the dimensions of your RV's beds before shopping for mattresses or bedding.

Sofa Beds

Sofa beds are typically made with lightweight but durable materials and can be stored away easily when not in use. Sleeping on these beds can be a bit uncomfortable for some, especially if the sofa in question has insufficient padding or is worn out. However, you can largely remedy these issues by investing in a quality mattress. These beds are also typically the least expensive option for RV owners on a budget, and they take up the least amount of space when not in use.

Bunk Beds

Another common type of bed in RVs, you're likely already familiar with bunk beds.

Just like sofa beds or any other type of bed you'll find in an RV, you can upgrade bunk beds with new mattresses. Remember, you'll need to make sure you know the correct sizes to buy. RV beds often require special mattress sizes.

Convertible Dinettes

Another common type of RV bed, the convertible dinette, is a large table that can fold down into a bed. These beds are typically not as comfortable as other types of RV beds, but they do have the advantage of seating up to four people around the table when it is in its upright position. Convertible dinettes also take up a substantial amount of space in an RV when not in use and are often quite heavy.

Overhead Bunks

Overhead bunks are most common in truck camper-style RVs and specific Class C motorhome designs. An iconic style of sleeping arrangement often found in vintage campers, an overhead bunk is set above the main area of an RV that can be reached by climbing a ladder.

Overhead bunks take up a good amount of vertical space in the RV, but not too much horizontal space. They are typically fit for one person, and the limited headroom does not suit all sleepers. However, this classic style of RV bed gives an RV a classic look that some owners prize.

RV Bathrooms

One of the essential parts of any home is the bathroom. If you are a frequent camper, then you probably know this all too well. When living in a small space such as an RV, the bathroom can be a bit of an issue. While RV bathrooms come in many different shapes and sizes, they all have their unique quirks that you need to be aware of.

RV Bathrooms—Water Pumps and Water Pressure

RVs use a water pump system to move water from the storage tank through the pipes and to the plumbing fixtures. Modern RV water pumps are electric, using your RV's 12-volt power supply to provide water pressure on demand.

In this case, "on-demand" means that the water pump will

activate automatically whenever the plumbing system requires it. If your RV has a water heater, it will direct water pressure there as needed and will otherwise send water directly into your RV's pipes. There should also be a switch to turn your water pump on and off manually, and some older water pumps may require manual activation whenever the pressure gets too low.

If your RV's water pump doesn't provide enough pressure, you can upgrade it to a more powerful pump. However, a water pressure regulator is essential in this instance to ensure the water pump doesn't supply more pressure than your RV's pipes and fixtures can handle.

When your RV is connected to an external water supply, you will not need the water pump to provide pressure.

RV Bathrooms—Wet Baths vs. Dry Baths

There are two basic types of RV bathrooms: wet and dry. These two types of bathrooms have their pros and cons, which are explained below.

Wet Baths

Wet baths are compact RV bathrooms typically found in smaller truck campers and trailers. These bathrooms include the typical bathroom fixtures of a toilet, a sink, and a shower, all located within the same space.

These types of bathrooms take up a minimal footprint in an RV's floor plan and are quite functional, but they do pose some disadvantages. The limited space makes it difficult for larger people to move around while using the facilities, and bathroom storage, in general, will be limited. It may also take some time for anyone accustomed to a traditional bathroom style (with a separate shower and toilet) to adjust to using a wet bath regularly.

Dry Baths

A dry bath in an RV is much closer to a traditional full bathroom found in a sticks-and-bricks style home. A dry bath typically includes a sink and a toilet with a separate shower stall.

These bathrooms generally take up more space than a wet bath but offer much more functionality and comfort. The primary drawback to dry baths is that they require more space, limiting the size and type of RV they can be installed in.

RV Bathrooms—Toilet Types

RV toilets come in a variety of shapes, sizes, and ways of functioning. Some types of RV toilets work similarly to the standard toilets found in most modern buildings, while others are quite different.

Composting Toilet

A composting toilet is a "dry toilet" designed to function without using any water. It receives and separates solid waste from liquid waste and uses a combination of materials and ventilation through aerobic decomposition until it can be used (as compost) or disposed of safely and correctly. These toilets are becoming increasingly popular as a replacement to the standard RV toilets due to water restrictions in many places and being more in line with a sustainable, ecologically friendly lifestyle.

These toilets don't flush and require no plumbing hookups, and if used and maintained properly, they store and break down waste and toilet paper in a way that's both safe and odor-free. However, they do need maintenance, and many of these toilets require replenishment with materials like sawdust or peat moss to control odors and help with safe decomposition.

Some composting toilets have an electric ventilation system, which will use some power. Finally, not all RVers or their guests will be comfortable with this type of system.

Cassette Toilets

Cassette toilets are commonly used in RVs, boats, and other places where you can't install a regular flush toilet. These toilets are self-contained units that don't require any plumbing hookups or external waste tanks. They use a small amount of water to fill the bowl, and then vacuum suction removes the waste.

Instead of emptying into a large tank that needs a special hookup for dumping, cassette toilets have their own built-in tank—the "cassette" part of the toilet—which you can easily remove to dump at a public bathroom when full.

Cassette toilets require a more straightforward hookup than traditional flush toilets and are a way to avoid the process of finding an RV dump station and emptying the black tank. However, cassette toilets will still likely need frequent emptying as well as thorough rinsing and cleaning. They also require a fresh water hookup.

Cassette toilets are a good choice for RVers who don't want to deal with the hassle of emptying a black water tank.

Gravity Flush Toilets

Flush toilets are the most common type of RV toilet. They work by using a fill valve to fill the toilet bowl with water, then flushing it away with a powerful surge of water. This type of toilet uses a lot of water and is not as easy to empty as a cassette or composting toilet.

This is where your RV's black tank comes into play.

RV Bathrooms—Emptying the Tanks

If you use a standard flush toilet, your black tank is where everything goes with each flush. Some RVs have "gray tanks" for water from the shower and sinks, while many are designed for everything to empty into the black tank. Either way, if your toilet flushes into a black tank, you will need to empty the sewage from this tank regularly.

Emptying the black tank is often intimidating for new RVers, but like everything else in the world of RV Living, the process of emptying this tank at a facility becomes easier with practice. If your RV has a gray tank, clearing that after the black tank will help remove any solids remaining in the sewer hose. You can use the same hose to emptying the black and gray tanks, but naturally, you'll need another hose to fill the fresh water tank. Heavy-duty RV sanitation gloves are more durable than disposable latex or vinyl gloves.

Your RV's Storage Room: Making the Most of It

Your RV is sure to come with a host of amenities, but storage space will always be at a minimum. The trick to successfully living life in an RV is organization, which is achieved through a combination of paring down, finding the best spots for the possessions you will bring with you, and getting into the habit of keeping everything in its proper place. The more you can do to keep your RV organized; the easier and more pleasant your life will be.

A good habit to get into from the start is keeping your area clean. Storing all of your items in a place where they can be easily found will not only keep your RV looking nice and tidy, but it will make finding things much more straightforward.

Keeping everything in a set place will also help you keep track of any new possessions you bring into your RV while you are on the road. In order to make space for anything new, you may first have to decide what to get rid of from your belongings so everything will fit. By keeping a set place for everything, it makes organizing everything much more manageable.

You can use several different methods to keep your RV organized. Some people prefer drawer organizers, shelves, closet systems, and the like, while others just use crates, boxes and duffel bags to pile their stuff in. Ultimately, whatever works best for you is what you should use.

If you prefer the simplicity of crates and boxes, a good idea is to get ones with lids. you can use them to store just about anything, from clothing and books to kitchen appliances and even office supplies.

A common method for storing clothes is using drawers. While an RV's drawers are great while on the go, an easier method is to simply use garment packing folders to fold everything and keep them stacked or hung neatly. If you prefer something with more structure, there are a multitude of drawer systems available for RVs that can easily be set up and taken down as you travel.

Alternatively, you could set up shelves to store your supplies. Stacking organizers are inexpensive, lightweight, and will hold just about anything from clothes to small tools and electronics to office supplies for more general storage.

You can also find several RV accessories with multiple uses, like a shoe rack that you can use in your bathroom to hang towels. Most RVs will come with a closet or dresser, so you should make use of these as much as possible.

One way to ensure that you're using any RV closet space to its fullest potential is to utilize efficient storage solutions like hooks and hanging storage to fit as much as possible into designated storage spaces.

You could also use some non-traditional methods to keep your clothes neat and organized. For example, there are several ways to store socks and underwear. You could buy a package of suspender clips from an office supply store and clip them inside your trousers or shorts.

For storing lighter items that may not fit in your closet or that you'd prefer to keep elsewhere for convenience, there is a simple, affordable solution that is a growing trend in the RV world: Magnets.

By attaching these magnets to your RV walls, you can then use metal storage boxes often found at office or home supply stores or even metallic containers made for a specific purpose (like magnetic spice racks) and store just about anything.

If you're not yet familiar with this trend, you'll find that home goods and discount department stores carry a surprisingly wide assortment of specialized magnet storage solutions made for these purposes.

You should also try to think outside the box, so to speak, when it comes to hanging things up in your RV and utilize space that you wouldn't usually think of. For example, if you've got an awning over your RV's entryway, you could use hooks to hang things like towels and wet shirts to dry while your RV is parked in an appropriate spot. Also, if you're near a shower facility while traveling or at an RV park with showers available, a shower caddy can be used to store your toiletries for quick access, and you can easily sling over it your shoulder.

And, of course, you could always utilize any spare areas on your RV's walls by using a pushpin board or any other method that allows you to safely affix items to the walls without causing damage. Suction cups, for example, work well for RV bathroom walls and can hold lightweight objects like shampoo and conditioner bottles.

Extra storage tips and tricks

If you're like most people, the area under your RV's bed is going to be reserved mainly for large, rarely used items. In this case, you'll need to make sure that everything stored there is adequately protected so that it doesn't get damaged from leaks or moisture. You may also want to consider using some sort of container or plastic to line the sides of the bed so that any items you store under there don't get dusty.

You'll also need to make sure that any items you store under your bed are secure. Make sure that nothing can move around freely under there. As an extra safety measure, you could even affix small bungee cords or elastic rope to the bottom of your bed and then loop them around each item to keep them from moving around.

You'll also need to think of the weight distribution when loading heavy items into the RV. For this reason, you should attempt to keep heavy items as low as possible in your RV if at all possible.

Chapter Summary

- RV sleeping arrangements come in various configurations, including standard beds, bunk beds, sofa beds, overhead bunks, and convertible dinettes. All of these options can be upgraded with the right mattress bedding, but make sure you shop for the right sized goods for your RV's setup.
- Common types of RV toilets include composting and cassette toilets, which do not empty to your RV's holding tank, and traditional flush toilets which do.
- An RV's sewage holding tank is called a black tank and needs to be emptied at designated dumping stations.
- RV bathroom types include wet baths, with toilet, shower, and sink all in the same compartment, and dry baths, which feature separate showers and a more traditional setup for those fixtures.

- Storage space will be at a premium aboard your RV, and some ways to make the most of it include stacked boxes, garment folders, magnets, awnings, and suction cups.

POWER AND CONNECTIVITY

Most new motorhomes come equipped with some sort of electrical or solar system and a place to plug in your Wi-Fi, computer, or access point. However, there is a chance you will want to replace or upgrade the power and connectivity options your RV may include. If you're buying a used RV or a non-motorized vehicle, you might need to start from scratch and install your own power generating and communications systems. This chapter will familiarize you with the options available and how to get the most out of them when you're out on the road with your RV.

RV ELECTRICAL SYSTEMS - THE BASICS

There are three major components to every motorhome that need electricity in order to run: the power source, the power converter, and the power outlets. It is crucial to be familiar with these terms to communicate more effectively with your technician and not get lost in a maze of techno-babble.

Electricity is provided by generators or the main power grid.

The power converter transforms the electricity from the power source into a form that your appliances can use.

Power outlets are the places where you plug in your appliances and recharge your electronic devices.

The RV power cord is what you plug into the electricity hookup at an RV park or campgrounds.

The three types of RV power sources are battery, shore power, and generators, with most of them running through your RV's battery system to power your household appliances.

Most RVs come equipped with at least one standard 120-volt power outlet (though some have more). These can are suitable for any of your run-of-the-mill appliances, like a lamp, a desktop computer, or even a microwave. Contemporary RVs should also have USB charging ports included with their wall outlet system.

Now that you have a good understanding of the parts of an RV's electrical system, it is time to explore the different types of electricity available to motorhome owners so you can make an informed decision on which features you want in your RV.

SHORE POWER:

Shore power is what you get from plugging your RV into an external source of electricity, such as at a campground or RV park. The electricity flows into your RV through a heavy-duty rubber cable known as a power cord. This power cord is plugged into an electrical outlet called a receptacle. A typical RV receptacle looks like this:

POWER AND CONNECTIVITY | 93

Shore power can be supplied through your local power company or from a large generator. The benefit of shore power is that you don't need to waste fuel to produce the electricity you need for daily use. It is similar to using electricity in a sticks-and-bricks style home, where you can run all of your appliances without worry. The part of your RV's battery system, which powers many of your electronics, will also charge while you're plugged into shore power, giving you more time before having to rely on external power again once you're charged up.

GENERATOR POWER:

You may also generate your electricity from a generator on-board your RV. In this case, you will not be connected to any external power source; instead, you will run the generator yourself and use the electricity directly without going through a converter. The advantage of running on your own generator is that it gives you the freedom to go wherever you want, instead of being limited to locations with external power sources. While you will generally have to rely on your RV's house battery system, discussed below, a generator will give you much more time on the road with your electronics.

However, generators need fuel to produce power. Most commonly this is gasoline, although some generators run on diesel or liquid propane. There are also "dual-fuel" generators that use both propane and gasoline.

RV generators also vary widely in price, capacity, and features. Some models are designed to be permanently installed to provide power to an RV's house electrical system, and others to be more portable.

If you have a generator, be sure to monitor the fuel levels and never run the generator inside of your RV or any other enclosed space.

RV BATTERY POWER

Motorized RV batteries typically have two different systems for operating both the vehicle and its electronics: the standard 12-volt DC power system and the 120-volt AC system for running the more power-hungry "house" electronics— your refrigerator, air conditioning, and anything else that needs more electricity than the 12-volt system can handle.

These batteries are traditionally lead-acid types, similar to what you would find in most cars on the road today. However, lithium-ion batteries are becoming more common in RVs, especially since they can work in tandem with solar panel systems. Since there can be two, four, or more of these batteries linked together in one rig, you can imagine that it takes quite a few to keep everything going, and they generally need to work with a generator or some other power supply for frequent recharging.

Typically, this battery system works with the shore power or generators discussed above to power your RV's electrical system.

If you're plugged into an external power source, such as shore power or a generator, then your RV's battery charger is only used for recharging the batteries when they are low on power. However, if you're not plugged in, the generator will kick on now and then keep your batteries from losing power completely.

You can upgrade these systems to longer-lasting batteries or, in the case of starting and running the RV, a propane or diesel generator can be used instead.

The 120-volt AC power system is pretty straightforward. It converts external AC power from the shore power cord or generator into usable DC power for your electronics, lights, and other things that require it. Some systems can do this through solar panels as well.

SOLAR PANEL POWER FOR RVS

While this isn't something that will supply all the power needed for every RVer, a small set of solar panels can be a great way to keep some basic power in your RV or camper while away from other power sources, supplement your existing power supply, and help cut down on your fuel usage and carbon footprint.

These are typically sold as supplemental power sources for RVs, with the ability to be tied into the RV's power supply when parked, or the panels can be linked directly into your RV's battery system and trickle charge the battery when the vehicle is in use.

While the somewhat limited usefulness and need to be parked in the full sun makes it less than an ideal primary power source, it can be a great secondary or backup option. A typical RV solar system consists of a set of panels, a charge controller, and the wiring needed for installation. They can usually be found online or at RV supply stores.

There are two types of solar panels on the market for RV solar kits: Monocrystalline and Polycrystalline. The main differences between the two are cost and efficiency, with monocrystalline panels being more efficient but also cost significantly more than their polycrystalline counterparts.

While it isn't a problem for most RVs, solar panels (especially monocrystalline) can still be somewhat fragile and susceptible to scratching; so make sure if you do get a kit that you take care when installing and handling.

Of course, safety is paramount if you're going to be doing any work on your RV's electrical system yourself. It is recommended that you turn off the main breaker before making any connections or alterations to your RV's power.

While there are countless tutorials, guides, and how-to guides for installing an RV solar kit online and elsewhere, the general idea behind it is relatively simple: The panels will be mounted on the roof of your RV, with wires running into the RV itself (or a storage compartment directly below in some cases) where the charging system is located.

POWER PACKS FOR RVS

An inexpensive solution that may be appropriate for some very low power usage situations or as an emergency backup, power packs are large battery banks that are charged using a generator or some kind of external power source.

Once charged, the power pack can be used to power smaller electronics and cell phones via USB or AC outlets. Heavier duty power packs have on/off switches and can be used for some heavier appliances or laptops, while lighter power banks are mainly intended for smartphones and other devices of that power caliber. While that might not be a solution for any significant power needs in your daily RVing, keeping a decent power pack on hand for emergencies is worthwhile.

In fact, some of these electricity storage devices are made especially for emergencies, with the built-in ability to produce some power via a small solar cell or even a hand crank.

RV CONNECTIVITY

For RVers in the 2020s, staying powered while on the road is just one part of the equation.

Over the past couple of decades, the internet's reach has extended far past wired home computers and is considered a necessity for daily life not unlike electricity.

The worldwide, high-speed connectivity allowed by the internet is now heavily utilized for cell phones, business operations, banking, shopping, and streaming entertainment. This has resulted in a far more widespread adoption of faster, more reliable internet than ever before.

Fortunately for RVers, the internet is now literally in the air like TV or radio signals, thanks to cellular and satellite data networks.

In practical terms, this means that it's becoming as easy to get online on the road as it is at home.

Just whip out your cell phone or tablet, and you can browse countless social media and news sites or watch movies and shows just like you would at home. You can even get a secure internet connection for your computer if you need to do some work or banking while out on the road.

Usually, that is. If you've ever tried to check your email on your phone while at a remote location, you know that things are not always quite that simple. While mobile internet coverage is getting better as major data carriers expand and upgrade their infrastructure, it's still not quite universal everywhere, yet. And depending on your carrier, your options for receiving mobile data on your phone may be limited, likely even more limited if you want to use that connection for your laptop and tablet as well, which is something you'll want in your RV as wired internet is not possible.

Luckily, there are options to stay as connected as possible while RV living. It's just a bit different from what you might be used to with sticks-and-bricks living.

This is due to a few different factors, including geography, climate, and land management. If you've ever tried using GPS regularly, then you already know that it can be spotty in certain areas. This is amplified when a satellite has to relay the signal from the remote location to a data center before sending it along to you. That's an extra step that sometimes can't keep up when demand is high, or the satellite can't find a clear path to where you are.

MOBILE DATA HOTSPOTS

Unlike your cell phone, which might have the ability to tether one or two other devices to its connection, a mobile hotspot device is specially designed to convert a cellular data signal into a robust Wi-Fi network for multiple devices.

These are also often more powerful than a typical Wi-Fi hotspot, allowing you to pick up a signal from farther away and through building material that might block it. The latest generations of mobile Wi-Fi hotspots can handle many devices, often ten or more.

Further muddying the distinction between a mobile hotspot you can take with you in your RV and a traditional Wi-Fi router attached to a broadband modem.

Any modern RV should have enough electrical capacity to run a laptop or tablet in addition to other devices like TVs or lights. Most RVs come with electrical systems that can easily handle one or two such devices without any trouble whatsoever, so this wouldn't be an issue no matter what you need the internet for.

Most major carriers do offer these hotspots along with data plans, including unlimited data plans. While this is likely to be pricier than wired broadband internet, these plans generally include messaging and voice calls covering your phone costs as well.

While this solution to having high-speed internet in your RV has many upsides, one thing to consider is that any mobile connection is prone to reliability issues when it comes to things like video streaming or teleconferencing, so keep this in mind if you're planning on relying on your connection for remote business conferences or for streaming music and movies wherever you are.

One tip if you have unlimited is to take advantage of a fast connection when you find one. For example, you can rent or buy some movies or TV show episodes from an online service and download them to your device to watch later when your connection might not be as strong.

If you don't plan to use the internet heavily, then a limited plan could be a way to save money. Some cheaper unlimited plans offer a limited amount of high-speed data followed by unlimited slower data once you hit that threshold.

For RVers who need more data, tethering is an option for phones that support it. This turns your phone into a hotspot of its own. You will need to check whether your carrier allows this for your data plan--or whether you can get an add-on for it--, but it only requires that you're able to get a strong enough signal where you'll be staying for the time being.

SATELLITE INTERNET

If you plan to spend most of your time in more remote locations, you might want to look into satellite internet plans instead. These work much differently than traditional broadband or even mobile hotspots.

The first thing you'll need is a satellite dish installed on the roof of your RV. This dish will be connected to some equipment inside your RV, which will send and receive data between the dish and the satellites in orbit.

This is unlike an internet connection from your phone or mobile hotspot, relaying a signal from the nearest cellular tower. In this case, your signal will be coming directly from outer space. This can slow things down quite a bit.

Of course, you can always set your satellite connection to a lower speed if you don't need that much bandwidth.

But assuming that you have an adequate plan along with a suitable dish and receiver, you won't need any outside equipment to connect to the web while at your campsite, assuming that you have electricity available.

Unlike a mobile hotspot, which is a standalone device, a dish-based satellite internet connection will require installation on your RV. There are receivers made for installing on vehicles, often with protective coverings. Unlike mobile hotspots, or your phone's own data connection, a mounted satellite connection cannot go with you, your family, and friends on adventures away from your RV.

On the other hand, satellite internet is still a relatively new, growing technology, and there are now some options for standalone satellite receivers that require no installation. As of this writing, these options are generally pricier and less powerful than a roof-mounted receiver, but as RV living continues to grow in popularity, we can expect this technology to improve and get cheaper, just as it has for cellular reception in rural areas.

OTHER INTERNET OPTIONS

In the case of both cellular and satellite internet connections, you will still need to be within a certain range of a tower or satellite, respectively.

Many RV parks offer Wi-Fi as an amenity, offering a potentially faster signal than mobile data with unlimited access for anyone renting a spot.

Please note the quality of the Wi-Fi at any RV park will vary greatly depending on how close you are to the router, how crowded the park is, and the park's internet connection.

You can also find local libraries, truck stops, coffee shops and other businesses that offer free or cheap Wi-Fi to their customers. Coffee shops, in particular, have become popular spots for setting up a laptop and spending a few hours enjoying the Wi-Fi.

While it is not as common as it used to be for these establishments to offer public computer terminals with internet access, you will still find stores and libraries with this option in some parts of North America. If there is some urgent reason you need to get online and you have no other options, a big-box electronics store will likely have some computers and smartphones on public display which are connected to the internet.

Naturally, the store would probably appreciate it if you made a purchase while you're there. Anybody for a new iPhone?

Chapter Summary

This is a brief summary of the basics of how to stay powered and connected while RV Living:

- RVs get their power from shore power, which is an external electricity connection, an onboard generator, or their battery systems.
- RVs have separate DC and AC battery systems onboard, with 12-volt DC batteries to start the engines and run typical vehicle electronics and 120-Volt AC battery banks to power the household outlets and electronics.
- Solar panels can also be used to provide some or all of the power for an RV's appliances.
- RV internet connection options include mobile hotspots, tethered hotspots from a mobile device, and satellite internet.
- Mobile hotspots act like a router, creating a Wi-Fi signal from a mobile data connection (i.e., 5G or LTE).
- Alternative internet options include Wi-Fi at RV parks, coffee shops, or publicly accessible terminals at libraries or electronics stores.

7

REPAIRS AND GENERAL MAINTENANCE

There are many things that can go wrong with an RV, just like with any other vehicle. This chapter will discuss the general types of problems you might encounter with your RV and how to fix them.

As with any vehicle, preventative maintenance is key to keeping your RV in good condition over the long term. If you take good care of your RV, a well-built motorhome or trailer should last you a decade or even longer.

PREVENTIVE MAINTENANCE TO SAVE YOU DOWN THE ROAD

First and foremost, you should change your RV's oil regularly and always use the weight of oil specified by the manufacturer. The same goes for the oil filter. If the old oil is dark brown or black and your engine uses a filter, chances are you're overdue for an oil change.

If your RV has a Gasoline (petrol) or Diesel engine, it's also essential to keep the fuel lines free of dirt and debris. This is easily accomplished by draining the tank and fuel lines each fall and replacing the fuel filter.

To keep your motorhome running in top shape and avoid unnecessary hassles in the future, your oil filter is only one of a handful of filters you'll want to change regularly.

The fuel, hydraulic and cooling system filters should also be inspected and changed regularly, depending on the manufacturer's recommendations and how much you drive your RV. As an added benefit, these can significantly improve the performance and lifespan of other parts of your RV's engine.

Well-maintained batteries are also a must for any vehicle, but especially RVs. These start the engine and power everything from interior lighting to the water pump. Depending on the size of your RV and the manufacturer's recommendations, you should inspect and clean your battery terminals, along with having them tested every few months.

It should go without saying that any parts that show damage, such as a leaking hose or cracked filter, need to be repaired or replaced as soon as possible.

It may be tempting to try to save a few bucks and clean these parts instead of buying new ones, but it's really not a good idea.

GENERAL RV MAINTENANCE - FLUSHING THE WATER SYSTEM

Flushing your RV's internal plumbing is key to keeping its water system clean and free of harmful mold and bacteria, as well as preventing clogs, stuck valves, and other problems.

You can flush out your fresh water tank by running all of your RV's taps while the fresh water tank is connected to an external water supply—often known as a city water supply in the RV world (which is just a generic term for municipal water).

Many RVers will also choose to sanitize their fresh water tanks at the same time.

The most common method is to use a small amount of household bleach—two to four ounces per gallon of fresh water, depending on the bleach's concentration—mixed in with a full tank of water before flushing the solution through your RV's cold water system. After flushing the system with the bleach solution, fill the fresh water tank again and let it sit for about 12 hours before flushing again. You may have to repeat the fresh water flushing a few times to rinse away any remnants of bleach, usually when the odor is completely gone.

Some water tank manufacturers have special products they recommend for sanitizing the tank, so make sure to check before using bleach or any other product.

This may seem like a hassle, but it's a relatively simple process that can go a long way in preventing the spread of diseases through your fresh water supply.

Your RV's gray and black water tanks may also have input valves for flushing individually using a municipal water source. The holding tank treatment you use should make the use of any additional cleansers unnecessary, although it's best to follow the manufacturer's instructions.

You can flush your gray and black tanks at any site with a water hookup and an outlet for sewer dumping available within close enough proximity—attaching one hose from the water source to the tank's flush inlet valve and your designated sewage hose to the output. To avoid contamination, do not use the same hose you use to fill your fresh water tank for flushing these tanks.

If your RV's black tank does not have a special valve, you can get a special hose extension called a tank rinser, enabling you to rinse the tank through your RV's toilet bowl.

However, if you're not using this method, it's best to keep the toilet valve closed while flushing your black tank to avoid the risk of sewage backing up into the plumbing.

You should drain and flush your black and gray water tanks at least once every two to three months and before and after long-term storage or traveling through wintry weather for an extended period.

GENERAL RV MAINTENANCE - KEEPING YOUR VEHICLE CLEAN AND MAINTAINED

Remember that you'll be living in your RV and depending on it to carry all of your worldly belongings. It's crucial that you keep it clean and well-maintained to avoid any unnecessary damage or accidents.

RV Exterior Cleaning

Most RV cleanings can start with a hose down of the exterior. It's best to start at the top and work down so gravity can help rinse the dirt away. If you start at the bottom, you will have to spend extra time cleaning any dirt which has streaked from the top, re-cleaning some of the same surfaces.

After hosing the vehicle's surface, loosening and removing some of the grime and dirt from the surface, you can wash the RV with a standard car wash soap or a special RV cleaning formula. Look for a product that is free of dyes, as these can discolor your

RV's finish over time. If you have stubborn dirt or grease on your vehicle, you may need to use a sponge and manual labor to remove it. Be sure to use caution around the windows, rubber seals, and other surface areas that you can easily scratch using an improper cleaning tool. Rinse the vehicle after cleaning it to remove all traces of the soap and dirt and make sure that the chemicals you used won't damage any painted or glossy surfaces.

If your RV has slide-outs, make sure to clean all of those surfaces as well, and remove any awnings before cleaning to make sure you don't leave any part of your vehicle's exterior uncleaned. Your awning itself may need a special cleanser, depending on its materials. Consult the owner's guide for the proper way to clean it.

RV Interior Cleaning

When tackling what may seem like the overwhelming task of cleaning every surface of your RV's interior, breaking the work down into different chunks can help make it seem more manageable.

For example, you can start by cleaning all the floors, including vacuuming any carpets or rugs, then move onto the cleaning which needs to be done in each room: cleaning the bathroom counters and fixtures, then the kitchen counters and the refrigerator, etc.

General RV Maintenance - Checking the Tires

Keeping your tires properly inflated is really important. Every RV owner needs to check their tire pressure at least once a month and adjust as necessary.

Most tires have a specific PSI, or Pounds per Square Inch that they need to be at to carry the vehicle's weight without risk of blowing. This is especially important when pulling heavy loads.

Most tires also have a warning label on the inside of the driver's side door that details how much weight the tires can safely carry.

The easiest way to check tire pressure is to use a tire gauge, which you can purchase at any automotive store for less than ten dollars. They look like a metal tube with a dial on one end. Place the metal tip on the valve, and make sure it is seated securely. Then, turn the dial to whichever setting corresponds with your tire size (this information should be printed somewhere on the side of your tire or in your user's manual).

When you press the metal tip against the valve, it should briefly hiss. Hold it there for a few moments to get your reading. If it is below the recommended tire pressure, inflate the tire and take another reading.

Continuing to drive on under or overinflated tires can cause irreparable damage, so it is vital to address the situation as soon as possible.

PREPARING YOUR RV FOR THE WINTER AND SUMMER MONTHS

There are a few things you can do during the spring and fall months to make sure your RV is ready for the winter and summer.

Winterizing Your RV

Winterizing your RV is especially important if you plan to store your RV during the cold weather months. However, suppose you're not planning to use your RV as often during the winter. In that case, it's still essential to de-winterize before and re-winterize after each use to prevent freezing until the warmer weather comes back around.

Winterizing helps prevent pipes from freezing and bursting, which can result in thousands of dollars worth of damage to your RV. Every RV is different, but the basic premise is the same. If you're not sure where your water pipes are, consult your owner's manual.

To start, drain all the water in your fresh water holding tank, then flush your black and gray tanks. This is an excellent opportunity to give them both a thorough clean. To ensure all the water is drained completely, flush your toilet several times and open the taps. There will still be a small amount of water left in the lines, it's best to remove this if you can to prevent the antifreeze from being diluted. An excellent way to do this is with a wet vac to suck out the remainder or, alternatively, an air compressor to blow it out. Next, re-cap any drains, close all open faucets and get your antifreeze to add to your water heater, plumbing pipes, and any other area where water flows. If you don't have a water heater bypass it's definitely worth fitting one. It will make the process much simpler and will save you an extra 6 gallons of antifreeze

Please note that the propylene glycol-based antifreeze meant for winterizing an RV's plumbing system is not the same as automotive antifreeze. Propylene glycol antifreeze is nontoxic and also acts as a lubricant, which helps to maintain the seals and pipes of your RV's water system.

There's also ethanol-based RV antifreeze, which is toxic and should not be used in your RV.

Now you will have to get the antifreeze into your RV's system. If your RV has a siphon hose on your water pump (you may need to check your user manual if unsure), you can simply connect it to your antifreeze and use it to get the antifreeze into your RV's plumbing system. If you don't have a built-in siphon, you can look into installing one. Or another option is to use a hand pump to pump the antifreeze straight into your city water inlet.

When your siphon valve is open, close your fresh water valve and turn on your water pump to fill your system with the antifreeze. Now go round your hot water taps in turn, turning them on until you see the antifreeze come through. Next, go through your cold water taps. This process will fill your lines with antifreeze, preventing them from freezing.

The amount of antifreeze you need for the entire RV will vary depending on the size of your lines, holding tanks, and whether or not you choose to bypass the water heater.

After the winter, you will need to flush your RV's plumbing system as described in the section below before adding any fresh water.

When storing your rig for the winter, you should also disconnect all of your electronics. Ensure your generator is off and disconnected, cover any exterior vents, and check to see if any cracks in the windows or doors need to be sealed.

It is also a good idea to remove your batteries and store them somewhere cool and dry. Do not let the temperature drop below 32°F (0°C) or exceed 80°F (27°C). You should make sure your batteries don't freeze.

A word of warning. Attempting to charge a frozen battery can be highly dangerous as it can explode.

If you do plan to stay in your RV during the winter, and you will be in areas where the weather dips below freezing consistently, there are some additional steps you can take to prepare for the winter.

The factory-installed heat source on your RV should be your goto as the heat ducts will be routed around the plumbing to prevent it from freezing in cold weather.

Until you get the hang of living in your RV during the winter months, it's a good idea to stay at a campsite that can provide you with electricity and facilities. This will give you the ability to use your onboard heating as and when you need it without having to worry about using up your batteries or generator fuel. This way, you can practice seeing how long these supplies last, then easily replenish them, knowing you can fall back on shore power at any time. The factory-installed heat source on your RV should be your goto as the heat ducts will be routed around the plumbing to prevent it from freezing in cold weather.

A heated water hose will also help prevent water from freezing and are easy to have installed. Using heat tape where lines are poorly insulated or exposed to the elements is also a good idea. If you're worried about your holding tanks freezing, you can also get tank heaters to combat this. Putting RV antifreeze down the toilet can also help keep things from freezing as a preventative measure.

However, if the weather does get extreme and is constantly below freezing, the best option may be to leave the fresh water system winterized. This will mean stocking up on water as you will have to use it for cooking, flushing the toilet, washing, and drinking. If you are at an RV park, you will no doubt be grateful for a hot shower!

Electric space heaters and electric blankets are also worthy investments for winter RV Living. Install sheets of plastic film over all of your RV's windows for extra insulation. Plastic insulation film is inexpensive and widely available at hardware stores.

Keep any curtains or blinds you have for your RV's windows closed as much as possible, and put a sunscreen in your RV's windshield when not on the move. This will help keep heat from escaping your RV.

All set? You're good to go until the fall!

PREPARING YOUR RV FOR HOT WEATHER

The temperature is rising, and so is the number of RV trips on the horizon. Whether you're taking a trip to the lake or going on an extended hiking trail, there are a few things you can do now to make your life a little easier later.

These are all important steps to take before embarking on a scorching summer of RV Living. If your RV has been in storage for the winter months, it is essential to flush away the antifreeze before adding potable water.

If your vehicle is subject to both extreme hot and cold temperatures during the year, it's not a bad idea to go through this process at least twice (for example, after the winter and a few months later when the summer heat starts picking up).

Flush and Sanitize Your Water System

An effective method to flush RV antifreeze is to connect your RV's water intake to the city

water tap or an outside tap if you are at home. Next, turn on all the faucets and open the gray tank. Keep flushing the water until it looks crystal clear and smells clean. If your water still smells of antifreeze after extensive flushing, treating it with baking soda should remove the remaining smell.

IF you have been using your RV through winter, this could be an ideal time to sanitize your RV's plumbing using the process we detailed earlier, as higher temperatures tend to breed bacteria. This will also give all of the parts a thorough inspection and let you know if any additional repairs need to be made before your trip, after a substantial time away from traveling, or at the start of the winter or summer season.

Check Your RV's Appliances and Electrical Systems

Swap out your RV's air filters and have the appliances serviced or replaced as needed. Check all of your fuses and electrical wiring. If you see any frayed wires, burnt-out breakers, or other signs of damage, have them repaired right away.

Test your refrigerator and, most importantly, your air conditioning to make sure they are running correctly. If something needs to be fixed, you'll want to get it done before the temperature rises, and you really need it.

It's best to do this while hooked up to shore power, if possible, in case there is an issue with your RV's internal electrical systems. A shore power connection will also give you the chance to charge your RV's batteries before setting out on summer adventures.

Check Your Fixtures and Water Hoses

You should also check your water hose for leaks and damage, particularly if you plan on using it for showers or with an outside water source. If you use a freshwater tank, check it for leaks or damage as well. This may require adding a dye tablet or two to thoroughly check for leaks.

Finally, give all of your showerheads, faucets, and other fixtures a good once-over to ensure they are all working correctly and ready for use.

Check Your Rig's Engine and Fluid Levels

Whether you have a motorhome or a trailer hitched to a truck, you should also make sure your vehicle is in good working order. Even if it seems to be running perfectly, you'll still want to give it a once-over before you set off. This includes making sure your oil and other necessary fluids are at their proper levels, your tires are properly inflated, and that there are no visible signs of damage.

If you haven't changed your oil or air filters for a while, an oncoming summer provides the perfect opportunity to do just that. The same goes for your water filter while you're at it.

Have you ever had your check engine light turn on mysteriously, and you keep forgetting to look into it? We've all been there, but when you know the summer weather is about to hit, you'll want to get that looked into as soon as possible.

Check Your Emergency Supplies

You should also check your emergency supplies and restock anything you've used. This includes extra water, blankets, batteries, clothing, and whatever else you included in your kits.

If you took the time to pack these items neatly away in a closet or box, it shouldn't take long to do a quick check and make any necessary replacements.

As you go through this short checklist, make a mental note of anything that needs to be repaired or replaced. Better to do it now when you've got time than to be caught off guard once summer has arrived.

Tailor this list to your own needs and the amount of time you have available before the summer heat hits. That way, you'll be able to get everything taken care of before you begin your season of RV Living.

And while this list may seem like a lot of work, it's much easier than dealing with the stress of being unprepared for the sudden onset of summer.

COMMON RV PROBLEMS: WHAT TO EXPECT AND HOW TO FIX THEM

Many of the problems you encounter in your RV will be minor. These can often be fixed quickly, so it's always best to know how to handle them. This is especially important if you're out in a remote area where help may take some time to arrive.

The following are some common issues you'll face while traveling in your RV and how to address them:

Common RV Electrical Problems

One of the most common problems that RV owners experience is a loss of power. This can be frustrating when you're in the middle of nowhere with no access to a mechanic or repair shop. Fortunately, there are several ways to troubleshoot and fix the problem yourself.

No Power to Your RV's Electrical Outlets

The first thing you should do is check the circuit breakers. Circuit breakers are designed to stop the flow of power in the case of a short or overload. If you've recently had a spike in power usage (such as when you turned on the microwave or hairdryer at the same time as another appliance), there's a good chance that this is the problem.

Your RV's outlets are likely on a separate circuit to the air conditioner and the water heater. If you're not sure which breaker controls the power to your outlets, try flipping them all until you find the one that restores power.

If you trip circuits frequently, you may be using more power than your RV's system can handle.

Blown Fuses

Blown fuses are another common problem with RV electrical systems. Although a blown fuse isn't as easy a fix as flipping a circuit breaker, it's not much more difficult or time-consuming.

A typical symptom of a blown fuse is a loss of power to the electronics that run on your RV's 12-volt system. This includes things like the lights and the built-in sound system.

RVs commonly have a fuse box located in the engine compartment or behind the dashboard, although sometimes the fuse box can be in an odd location. If you're not sure where it is, consult your owner's manual.

You can find instructions for replacing fuses in your owner's manual or on a sticker on the inside of your fuse box. Look carefully at the fuses in the box and their transparent glass windows. The blown fuse will appear gray or black.

Always make sure you're using the correct fuses for replacement. Fuses are designed to fail safely and prevent overheating of wiring or electrical devices from causing a fire. This is meant to protect you and your RV, and replacing a fuse with a higher amperage one is dangerous and can lead to a fire.

If you need to replace a fuse, be sure to use the correct one. The sticker on your fuse box will tell you what size fuse you need.

Tips for Avoiding RV Electrical Problems

1. Avoid Overloading the System - Your RV's electrical system consists of a series of breakers and fuses designed to shut down power to the system in the case of an overload. This is a good thing, but it also means you should never try to add more electricity to your RV than it was designed to handle.

If you try to run too many electrical appliances at one time or for too long, you can cause severe problems with your battery, wiring, and other electrical components.

2. External Hookups with an Outlet Tester - You should always test your external power supply before hooking up to it. This includes the power cords and the receptacle, which is the outlet on your RV.

If you're plugged into a campground or some other form of external power, use an outlet tester to make sure the power is on and working as expected.

These testers are inexpensive and easy to use. Once you plug it into the external power hookup, it will display any problems with the wiring, such as reverse polarity.

Reverse polarity especially can damage your RV's wiring and can even spark a fire, so it's imperative to test before plugging in.

3. Know Your Setup - Before you start RV Living in earnest, you can avoid many potential issues by familiarizing yourself with your RV's electrical systems and how to use them. This includes things like the location of the circuit breaker and the fuse box, knowing which appliances are on which circuit, and knowing whether your power cord has a 30-amp (3 prong) or 50-amp (4 prong) plug so you know which receptacle to use when you hook up to shore power. The few minutes it will take to learn these things about your rig will save you countless headaches and help ensure that your time RV living is as enjoyable and stress-free as it should be.

4. RV Roof Leaks - Another common problem you may face is a leak in the roof of your RV. This can be caused by various issues, including extreme weather, wear and tear, and even a poor design on the part of the manufacturer.

You may need to climb up onto the roof to ascertain where the water is getting in. Anywhere the manufacturer has had to cut into the external skin of the RV (lights, windows, vents etc.) can be a potential leak. Once you've found the spot, you can use a specialized patching product to seal the opening.

The product you use will be determined by the makeup of your vehicle's roof—rubber RV roofs have special patching kits and fiberglass roofs call for another kind of material. It's best to have these on hand before a problem arises.

This is usually a temporary fix, but it'll prevent any further damage to your vehicle until you have time for a more permanent repair.

5. Sinks, Showers, and Toilets Don't Work - If your RV's sinks, showers, or toilets suddenly stop working, there's a good chance that the problem is a clog in the system. This can be frustrating to fix because of their locations, but it's doable for even the most novice mechanics.

For minor clogs that you can identify as being near a sink drain or a toilet, a plunger may be all that's needed. In some cases, even boiling water can clear up blockage near a sink.

For more severe blockages, a plumbing snake can go a long way, literally. RV's with built-in plumbing will often have an access panel for repair work, but you won't necessarily need that if you're able to solve the clog with a simple plumbing tool like a plunger or snake.

Common RV HVAC Problems

There are fewer more frustrating feelings for an RVer than switching on your air conditioner on a hot summer's day and feeling hot air coming through the vents. Or even worse, no air.

However, this issue doesn't necessarily mean your HVAC system is broken or needs serious repair.

Even if you recently switched your air filter, it can still accumulate enough dust and debris that it needs to be cleaned (if reusable) or replaced under certain conditions.

This is usually an easy fix, and as soon as you turn your air conditioning back on, you'll know If that was the culprit.

After living in your RV for a time, you will start to grow quite familiar with your vehicle and its quirks. Not only will routine maintenance and minor fixes get easier with practice, but you'll start to get a sense as to when something is even slightly off.

This means you'll get better and better at identifying small problems before they become larger ones, and you'll get better at taking care of them and your home on wheels, as well.

Chapter Summary

Below is a brief summary of the most important RV maintenance tips and common problems:

- Necessary preventative maintenance includes flushing the plumbing system, checking the electrical system and appliances, checking the engine and fluid levels, checking the tires, and changing all of the filters.
- Thorough interior and exterior cleaning are also

important periodic measures for maintaining a safe and healthy RV.
- Common RV problems include electrical issues, which may be solved by checking the circuit breaker or changing a fuse.
- Roof leaks, which can be remedied temporarily with proper patching material.
- HVAC issues, which are frequently the result of a dirty filter which is an easy fix.
- You can avoid a vast majority of RV Living headaches through preventative maintenance as well as simple measures like not overloading the electrical system and testing the outlets at power hookups.

8

MAILBOXES AND HEALTHCARE

Whether you are traveling across the country or just staying within your own state, one thing that you will have to do at some point is communicate with people.

One of the most convenient and frustratingly inconsistent aspects of RV life is mailing out and receiving mail. While on the surface, this seems like a downside to RV living, like so much about RV Living, it also opens new avenues of perspective and appreciation of even the mundane facets of daily life.

When you're on the road, getting mail is exciting. Even a bill can feel exciting when you know it's from a place you've been and memories of the time you had there.

This chapter will cover the ins and outs of mailing from an RV and what you need to know about receiving mail during your time as an RV owner.

Getting Mail on the Road: Dealing with the US Postal Service (USPS)

If you live in the US, in a traditional sticks-and-bricks setting, there's a decent chance that your experience with the country's official postal service has been limited to receiving mail at an established postal address and maybe some visits to a local USPS location to buy stamps or send a package. However, establishing an address and receiving mail on the road will mean becoming more familiar with various USPS services than most of the country's residents.

One of the most important things to realize about the USPS is that there are many different types of USPS locations. From big post offices to small subcontractor locations and everything in between. The types of services available at each site vary greatly, so it's important to find the right one for you.

For the most part, mail will be received at a USPS mailbox. This can be a free USPS mailbox or one that you have to pay for.

The free option would be to receive mail at a residential address. If you're only RV living part-time and maintaining a US residence, that seems like the obvious way to continue receiving mail.

If you have a house sitter or somebody else who's willing to take in your mail while you're away, this could work quite well. Otherwise, you will need to find a paid solution to keep your mail from piling up.

This includes a rented post office box at a USPS location, or a similar mail and package receiving box at a UPS or FedEx location. Usually, USPS post office boxes are cheaper, but larger PO boxes require a higher monthly charge, and you will need a box that's large enough to hold everything sent to your official address until you can be there to pick it up.

While weighing your options, consider how often you'll be in the area to pick up any mail sent there. You can mitigate this by having your mail sent somewhere you know you will be when it arrives, and we'll look into this a bit more later in the chapter.

After finding a location and filling out an application, you will be given a unique key for the box, which will most likely be a numerical code. You can also set up a free USPS service called Informed Delivery which will send images of every piece of mail you're receiving to your email each morning. If you don't have a cell phone or any other device that can receive text messages or emails, make sure the PO box location offers another way to be contacted in case mail arrives while you're unavailable to accept it in person.

Suppose you are planning on living in your RV full-time and will no longer have an established address. In that case, a PO

Box might look like an easy solution to keeping an established residence for legal reasons and to collect correspondence. Unfortunately, a post office box, whether through the USPS or a private company, is not considered a legal address in any US state.

Some services will not only receive but also open and send you scans of all your mail for a monthly fee. These services are commonly known as virtual mailboxes or mail scanning services, and they provide you with a street address for all your mail.

Some of the more elaborate virtual mailbox services will also deposit any checks you receive, forward packages to an address of your choosing, and give you a choice whether to scan, shred, or forward each piece of mail.

Even with a virtual mailbox and an affiliated address, you will still need to establish a residency to have a driver's license and keep your RV insured and legally registered.

If you know you will be at a location for a long enough window to receive mail there, you can take advantage of a USPS service called General Delivery. With General Delivery, you can receive letters addressed to your name at a participating post office.

According to the USPS.com website, the address is usually something like Your Name, General Delivery, City, State, Zip Code.

Not every post office participates, and you need approval from the postmaster for a General Delivery account. You may be able to get approval ahead of time by calling the post office and asking to speak with the postmaster or the officer in charge.

Every USPS post office has somebody working in this capacity, although they may not be available when you call. You may have better luck using the directory on USPS.com to learn the postmaster's name before contacting the location.

That post office will hold your mail for up to 30 days, and you will not be able to receive parcels from any non-USPS service for general delivery. The good news is this service is free for US citizens.

While this General Delivery is a stopgap measure, you may be able to receive some mail while RV Living. For the reasons discussed above, you will need to establish a residence to have a legal address.

Getting Mail on the Road: Establishing a Residential Address in the US

One ostensibly easy method of establishing residency and having an official address is to use the address of a friend or family member.

Officially, you will be sharing your address with whoever this is, and they will be receiving all mail and packages sent to that address—unless you rent a box for this elsewhere.

This is, of course, a lot to ask of somebody.

If you are able to arrange this with somebody, that address is going to determine a lot about your life, even if you're RV Living full time.

In the US, the state and locality of your address will determine things like state and local taxes, voter registration (as well as the initiatives and many of the candidates on your ballot during elections), your vehicle registration, bank account options, health insurance options and more.

Maybe the most limiting factor you'll run into when choosing an official state of residence or domicile is that most states require you to live in a fixed residence– not an RV— inside the state's borders for a significant portion of the year (183 days is typical) to establish domicile.

Not all states require this, though. Some states don't have anything close to this annual requirement, such as Texas, Florida, and South Dakota.

There's a reason so many RVers have mailing addresses in one of those three states, and it isn't just the nice weather or the famous national parks with RV facilities within their borders.

These states do not have as strict requirements as many others regarding having a fixed home or spending time each year to establish a domicile.

South Dakota has the laxest requirements of any state as far as physical presence is concerned, requiring only one night in the state every four years. And yes, this includes a night in an RV park. South Dakota has no state income taxes, which will simplify your tax filings every year (or every quarter if you're a freelancer).

Texas requires your presence at least once a year for a vehicle inspection, but it has a well-established community of RV nomads and, like South Dakota, does not collect state income tax.

Florida does not collect income tax, either, and does not have a residency requirement before establishing domicile. While you will need an address in the state as part of the process, there are services that will help you with that part.

Each of those states is also home to multiple private companies established to help RVers establish domicile and receive mail.

However, when you establish domicile in a state, even those big three popular with RVers, you will be a resident of that state.

You'll need to visit to get your new driver's license and register your vehicle there—which will have that state's plates wherever you go. You will need to pay taxes there, and to vote, you'll need to register with the county of your domicile address.

You will need to file an affidavit with the state in question to establish domicile. It would be best if you cut all official ties to your previous state of residence—you don't want tax authorities from your last state thinking that you're still living there tax-free.

Even if you only visit once every few years, the state you choose will be your new "home."

Not your residence, but your domicile.

Escapees is one of the most extensive services to help RVers establish domicile and live an untethered lifestyle. They have more information on their website about what establishing domicile entails. Even if you don't wind up using their service, that information is worth reading.

Escapees or any established company which provides such services will help with all of your questions about the requirements for each stage, including how to handle issues like jury duty and legal challenges from your former state or the state where you're establishing domicile.

They may also be able to provide information on where to get an inexpensive mailbox and how to handle issues like continuing education credits or license renewals.

Health Insurance and Healthcare While RV Living

The nomadic lifestyle of an RVer can feel like freedom from many of the usual stresses and challenges of daily life, with the open road offering a constant fresh sense of perspective around every corner.

However, just like your RV needs proper care and maintenance for a long and healthy life, even the most independent and rugged of RVers need to take care of themselves as well.

While you may not need a traditional house or even to pay property taxes and can save money on gas, food, and entertainment costs, there are still some expenses that need to be factored into your travel budget.

For many full-time RVers, part of that cost often comes in the form of health insurance and healthcare expenses.

Fortunately, there are a few options available to help you keep these costs as low as possible while you're out on the open road.

If you happen to have a remote corporate job as an employee, your employer likely offers a healthcare plan that covers your basic needs and will save you from financial catastrophe if you run into any problems that require hefty medical bills.

If you're among the majority of RVers who do not fall into that category, there are other options.

As of this writing in 2021, the Affordable Care Act is still in effect, and there is an open enrollment period each year. During this time, you can log into the Healthcare Marketplace to shop for a plan that fits your needs.

These plans are not only less expensive than what you may have paid in the past, but they also offer enhanced benefits and protections.

These options, however, including Medicaid or Medicare if you qualify, will vary by your official state of residence or domicile.

If you're RV living full time, your coverage will be tied to the state in which you live and spend most of your time.

Because the state or province in which you register your vehicle is the one that will be considered your resident for insurance and healthcare purposes, it's essential to understand the rules about full-time residency for the areas where you spend most of your time.

Even if you've established a domicile in a state with relaxed requirements for the time you need to spend there, your health insurance company may not be quite as flexible.

Some companies and plans require you to live half the year at your residence, and some exclude RVers altogether.

While many insurance plans indeed have some sort of restrictions that make them less than ideal for RVers, there are a few insurance companies with plans geared explicitly towards mobile living.

The RVer Insurance Exchange and RVHealth.com are two places to research what your options might be. RVer-specific plans may be pricier than those offered directly through the Healthcare Marketplace, and every plan offers different advantages and disadvantages for each individual, so it's important to take a wide-ranging approach to your research.

Staying Healthy While RV Living

Even with a great health insurance plan, your primary care physician and your regular specialist doctors may be hundreds or even thousands of miles away. You may be traveling through remote areas without easy access to any substantial medical services.

These are some of the reasons it is imperative to pay attention to your health on the road. The happiness afforded by a life on the road provides some small measure or prevention, maybe, but diet and exercise are significant, too. Luckily, RV living presents plenty of opportunities for exercise and maintaining an active lifestyle.

Getting Exercise While RV Living Full Time

1. Hiking - For many RVers, there's no better way to work up a healthy sweat than taking a long walk or hike. RVers can choose from a vast variety of hiking trails in the United States and Canada, even Mexico, if you feel like making the drive to the border. These are available to enjoy all year-round.

Many of America's most popular and scenic hiking trails are located in rugged, mountainous terrain and offer spectacular views.

The Appalachian Trail, Pacific Crest Trail, and Continental Divide Trail are just a few of the great hiking trails that wind through America's famous National Parks.

The National Park Service has excellent resources and information for prospective hikers, as do many state parks.

2. Biking - If you happen to be carrying a bicycle or two with you in your RV, then you're set for some great road trips. RV parks are often located alongside or near popular biking trails, and many RVers enjoy biking along the shoulders of highways and through state and national forests.

Whether you're interested in road bikes or mountain bikes, there are trails for all skill levels and preferences throughout the country.

3. *Yoga* - Yoga is free, requires very little space, and no expensive equipment, making it a convenient way to work out, stay fit and give you a break from the rigors of RV life.

There are many different types of yoga, and a quick online search will help you decide which style is right for you.

Many local yoga studios offer drop-in classes, and the range of yoga classes to choose from in any given area is growing as the practice increases in popularity.

Yoga is a great way to keep your mind and body in shape no matter where you are in life.

Chapter Summary

This is a brief summary of the basics of receiving mail and staying insured while RV Living in the US:

- Options for receiving mail on the road include a PO Box, a virtual mailbox service, using a friend's or relative's address, or USPS General Delivery. However, you'll need a legal address no matter what.
- Even with no physical residence, you can use a service like Escapees to establish domicile in a US state with looser requirements for maintaining a legal address. However, that state will be your official home, and all of your legal business will be conducted there.
- Health insurance options for US RVers include plans purchased through the online Healthcare Marketplace, Medicare, or Medicaid if eligible.
- Unique private healthcare plans are also available for RVers.
- Health insurance can be geographically limited for the doctors and specialists you can see, so you might have to pay special attention to these restrictions when choosing a plan.

9

CAMPING AND BOONDOCKING

While full-time RV Living is often described as a life on the road, even the most nomadic and wanderlust-prone RVers need to pull over and take a rest sometimes.

Whether you just need a place to stop for a few hours sleep, or a spot to set up shop with your RV for a more extended break before hitting the road again, in this chapter, we'll go through some of the options you'll have for parking and staying with your RV.

Campsites for Your RV

Finding the perfect campsite is part of the adventure for many RVers.

When it comes to campsites, everyone has their own preferences--some like them secluded, others like them right next to the fun.

We're going to break down some of the significant campsite types and explain what you can expect at each one.

NATIONAL PARK SERVICE SITES-

The National Park Service (NPS) runs more than 1,420 different campgrounds, making this an excellent resource for RV owners.

There is often a fee to use the sites managed by the NPS, and these fees can vary between campgrounds. There is frequently a limit on the time you can camp in your RV at an NPS campground, with an average range of time between about two weeks to two months. Some NPS campgrounds have full hookups with dumping stations, while others simply have the space for a few smaller RVs.

However, many of the best national parks in the US, from Death Valley to Joshua Tree to Smoky Mountains, have space for you to park your RV and make your home for a while in the thick of some of the planet's best natural space.

The first place to start researching national park campsites is at the official NPS.gov website. This site has detailed information on general NPS rules and sections on each national park campground and the sites available for RVers.

RV PARKS

The other main type of location for RV owners is RV parks.

These are privately owned properties that offer RV parking and access to some or all of the following:

- Swimming pools and other recreational activities
- Wi-Fi
- Dump stations
- Convenience stores

There are many types of RV parks, from private to public to state parks. The similarities between these three types are that they all offer a place to park your RV and hookups for water, sewage, and electricity.

Each comes with its own unique set of rules and regulations that you should be aware of before signing a contract or paying money.

However, these types of accommodations for your RV can come in very handy as a way to take some time off the road and give your rig a rest from wear and tear while recharging your electrical system, dumping your holding tanks, and doing other needed maintenance.

These RV parks are much more common than national parks or other similar campsites for your RV, making them a convenience worth considering.

Urban Camping

One unique way to enjoy the RV lifestyle is to embrace an urban area and all the culture, sights and sounds it has to offer.

This type of RV lifestyle gives you easy access to towns and cities with all of their modern comforts while still allowing you to camp in relative safety, sometimes just a few blocks from a police station.

If you are a fan of RV Living but aren't always a fan of the "roughing it" approach that some RVers embrace, finding an RV park within a city— and there are more of those than you might think– may be the proverbial Goldilocks situation for you.

Camping out in your RV in a city can also be a nice change of pace if you want to take in a bit of all the country has to offer.

For example, you can stay for a while at the Liberty Harbor RV Park in Jersey City, NJ, with views of the Statue of Liberty and the Manhattan skyline through your window. When you're finished with your stay there, you can take a 90 minute drive through the breathtaking scenery of the Hudson River valley to the Catskills RV Resort in upstate New York for some more classic nature-oriented camping.

The country is dotted with RV parks, so finding one that fits your needs and budget is easy.

BOONDOCKING

In the RV world, "boondocking" can have a couple of different meanings, but overall it refers to finding a spot to camp your RV overnight or longer that is not necessarily designed for RVs and doesn't offer the amenities of an RV park or campsites intended for that purpose.

For some RVers, any place to camp with your RV without water, power, or sewage hookups is a type of boondocking. More specifically, staying at this type of campsite is known as "dry camping."

For others, the essence of boondocking is finding a free spot to stay with your RV, "free" being the operative word.

However, what unites all definitions of boondocking is that they all involve staying somewhere not designed specifically for RV camping or parking.

This style of camping requires a bit more planning and safety measures than traditional RV travel. It also requires a fair bit of experience and knowledge about which sites are legal to use and the peculiarities of various kinds of boondocking spots.

Boondocking: Where to Start

Before embarking on your boondocking adventure, you'll need to know exactly where you can go.

With the internet, there are communities like Campendium, which has a large section detailing free RV campsites on public lands in North America.

There is also information about a trickier yet potentially more accessible type of boondocking: staying with your RV in a commercial parking lot—as you would find outside a Walmart or truck stop—overnight.

We'll go through a couple of those basic types of boondocking here.

Boondocking: National Forest Service Sites

A good place to start is the National Forest Service (NFS), a United States government agency that manages the nation's forests.

Unlike the National Park Service, the NFS allows for dispersed camping--this means choosing your spot and setting up camp anywhere in the national forest, as long as you're not within the vicinity of any established campgrounds and at least 100 feet away from any streams or water sources.

The NFS also requests that RVers stay out of the path of established roads while boondocking, which seems like solid advice.

There is a 16 day limit per month for dispersed camping on NFS lands, and the service's Leave No Trace policy dictates that you clean all debris and leave your campsite the same as you found it.

Boondocking on NFS land is very much "backcountry" style camping with no amenities. You'll be responsible for providing all of your water, and the only restroom facilities will be whatever you have on your RV.

While you are likely to find natural water sources such as streams or lakes nearby while boondocking on NFS land, this water is very likely to be unsafe to drink.

It is safer and easier to stock up on water from a safe source beforehand, either bottled or tap from a nearby public facility. Some more well-traveled NFS sites have basic amenities such as public washrooms available, but those are the exception.

Boondocking: Parking Lots

Parking lots abound the world over, especially throughout the US and Canada. Many of them sit mostly or entirely empty overnight, with ostensibly plenty of space for you to park your RV for a few hours of rest.

Of course, it's not that simple when a vast majority of these lots are on private property, with many property owners considering unauthorized access to be trespassing.

While boondocking at a parking lot overnight is often a risky proposition at best, there are some notable exceptions– including one particularly massive discount department store chain.

Wal-Mart's store-wide policy on RV parking is well known in the RVing community and even published in the FAQ section of their official website.

As a rule, Wal-Mart allows for RV parking in their lots. However, the management, or the security, at a Wal-Mart location may or may not agree with this policy. The Wal-Mart website suggests asking the store manager beforehand, and local laws against overnight parking may well supersede store policy.

Other large chains which are generally friendly towards boondockers include Costco and Cracker Barrel.

You can find more information about these stores, individual locations, and other resources for boondockers at online boondocking communities like BoondockersBible.com and RV-Camping.org, as well as the official National Forest Service website at fs.usda.gov.

Chapter Summary

Here is a brief overview of the world of RV camping and boondocking in the US.

- You can find RV campsites with electricity and

plumbing hookups throughout the country in national parks and campgrounds as well as for-profit RV parks. You will usually have to pay for such spots.

- Some national parks have free RV camping for limited time periods. RV camping at any of these places may or may not require reservations.
- Boondocking is staying in your RV in a spot that does not offer RV-centric amenities such as plumbing or power connections.
- Usually, boondocking is free, and it can take many forms, from backcountry camping on National Forest Service grounds to staying overnight in a Walmart parking lot.
- Some large chain businesses, like Walmart and Cracker Barrel, have corporate policies sympathetic to boondocking, and you can often use their parking lots for overnight stays. However, store management and local laws may not be as sympathetic so remember to check with the store manager beforehand to avoid disappointment.

SAFETY AND WELL-BEING

With the proper precautions and knowledge, RV Living is a largely safe activity. This chapter will outline a few important steps to ensure that your enjoyment isn't interrupted by something unexpected.

The first thing you should do is familiarize yourself with your RV and the equipment that comes with it. Reading this book is a great start, but you'll also want to familiarize yourself as much as possible with the details and quirks of your particular rig.

Your owner's manual and any warranties you have for the RV or its parts will be of utmost importance if something breaks while you're traveling.

If you're not accustomed to driving a vehicle the size of your RV, you will want to have plenty of practice before setting out on your journey to be certain that you're comfortable with driving it and that you know how to handle it in various situations.

Many modern RVs have backup cameras, but even if that's the case with your vehicle, you will want to be confident in your ability to drive using only the mirrors and no rear window to see through, in case your equipment glitches or your camera simply stops working while on the road.

Apart from being familiar with your rig and how to drive it, along with much of the other preparedness advice we've gone through previously in this book, it's also a good idea to go through your insurance options before embarking on your RV Living odyssey.

RV Insurance

Getting insurance for your RV is not quite the same as getting basic insurance for your car.

RV insurance is specialized and vital for your peace of mind that if something goes wrong with your rig, it will be covered.

If you own a recreational vehicle, you'll want to protect its contents as well as your RV itself against damage, fire, theft, and other common perils.

Most standard auto insurance policies don't cover RVs or their contents, so you have to get a particular policy if you want that extra protection.

It's easy to do and relatively affordable if you do some shopping around for a plan that works for you.

If you're happy with your current auto insurance company, that's a great place to start looking into RV insurance. Most major insurance companies offer some policies specialized for RVs, with some having more extensive offerings than others.

Just be sure that whichever policy you choose covers your rig and your needs.

Some basic policies only cover your RV and its parts against fire and lightning damage, while others offer assistance in the case of theft.

You may also want to consider optional coverage for things like emergency roadside service, trip interruption insurance, and even total replacement cost for custom parts or equipment attached to your RV.

Another thing to keep in mind is special RV-related endorsements that you can add to your standard auto insurance.

For example, if you have a slide-out or a built-in device like an awning or roof rack, your traditional auto insurance may not cover these types of add-ons, so you'll need to have endorsements on your policy to make up the difference.

Some companies specialize in RV insurance, like Good Sam and National General, which offer more comprehensive RV-only policies.

These policies are more expensive than those offered by standard auto insurance companies, but they offer a wider range of benefits, such as roadside assistance and discounts at select campgrounds and RV parks.

No matter what type of RV you own or how you choose to insure it, you should take time to understand your policy and all of the fine print before hitting the road.

RV Safety - Mistakes to Avoid

As exciting as RV Living can be, it's important to remember that safety should be a top priority. With the nature of RV living, it's impossible to predict how close you will be to a hospital or any sort of medical care at any given time.

A small mistake while driving your RV down the road could result in a severe accident, so it's important to keep an eye on your surroundings and stay alert.

Here are some common RV mistakes to avoid:

Driving While Tired

It seems like an obvious one, but driving while tired is extremely dangerous, regardless of what vehicle you're in.

If you're planning on driving a long distance, make sure to take plenty of rest stops and don't hesitate to stop at a campsite early if you start to feel sleepy.

Speeding / slow and steady wins the race

Obviously, this is not a safe practice for driving any vehicle on public roads, but it's especially risky to go fast in an RV. An RV is a much larger vehicle than a typical sedan or SUV and, because of this, it takes more time to slow down and stop than a car would.

You should also be aware that state and local authorities have different speed limits for large vehicles like RVs and that speed is always slower than the limit for cars.

Unlike driving a car, you can't rely on posted signs to know the local speed limit for your vehicle. This is another arena where a good GPS—especially an RV-specific GPS—along with research of the areas you'll be visiting will come in handy.

Driving in Poor Weather

Another primary safety concern is driving your RV in poor weather conditions. During the winter months, it is crucial to stay on top of the weather conditions and forecasts wherever you'll be traveling.

Of course, no matter how well informed you are, inclement weather can come out of nowhere. So it's always best to be prepared and carry a few supplies with you at all times.

Things like extra water, blankets, warm clothes, emergency food, and a fully charged cell phone are always good to have on hand. This list might seem like common sense, but these items are significant enough to warrant mentioning.

If your RV has a satellite radio, it can also be used in the event of an emergency.

Not Minding Your Clearance

In a typical passenger car, SUV, or even a pickup truck, you rarely, if ever, have to think about clearance—that is, the height of your vehicle and whether you can make it safely beneath underpasses and through tunnels.

However, the motorhome or trailer you're driving may be tall enough that you'll need to start paying attention to avoid serious damage to your vehicle or worse.

The height of your vehicle is best measured yourself rather than taking the manufacturer's or dealer's numbers as entirely accurate. You'll also want to account for any air conditioners or satellite dishes on the roof.

This is another spot where an RV-specific GPS will come in handy, as they will often have warnings about low clearances (below 14 feet or so) on various routes. In the US, the Federal Highway Administration enforced a rule that all underpasses must be at least 14 to 16 feet tall on highways.

However, you can't always rely on the posted height of any underpass to be reliable. It's wise to subtract two feet from the posted height to be on the safe side and go slowly if it will be a tight fit.

The best way currently to minimize your chances of getting stuck is to use a good RV GPS and/or one of several mobile apps made specifically to help drivers with larger vehicles find the best route. These apps include TruckMap and CoPilot RV.

Driving an RV is a rewarding and fun experience for everyone. By keeping safety in mind, you can make sure that it stays that way!

RV Security Precautions

Whether you're planning on RV Living full time or just a portion of the year, while you're traveling or parked your RV, is your home.

As such, it should be secured. This includes keeping your vehicle locked, especially while you're away or sleeping inside, keeping any valuables out of view of the windows, investing in a steering wheel lock, and using other appropriate security devices—such as an alarm system.

Locking Your RV

Most recreational vehicles are parked and left unattended at some point. As a result, the vehicle can become a prime target for theft or vandalism. While it's important to remember that you shouldn't keep valuables in your vehicle, there are other things you can do to make your RV less of a target and lessen the impact if it is broken into.

When you're not using your vehicle, it's a good idea to park it in a well-lit area where there is a lot of activity. If this isn't possible, think about investing in high-quality motion-sensing lights and placing them around the outside of your vehicle.

Ensure all windows are closed and locked before going into a store or setting out on a trip.

RV Security Systems and Anti-Theft Measures

Just like home camera security systems, security systems for RVs have become increasingly popular in recent years as the price for these systems has gone down, and technology has allowed for easier and more efficient monitoring.

There are a number of different security cameras on the market designed especially for RV use. These cameras can be installed both inside and outside of the vehicle. Most are capable of sending their signal to a monitor inside your RV, or to your smartphone or another mobile device while you're away from the vehicle.

Security Cameras

As your RV will be your part-time or full-time home on the road, you can protect it similarly with a home security system. Modern security camera systems connect remotely to a stream you can monitor from your smart device, so you can check in on it while you're away.

Systems are also available to alert you if they detect any movement or external factors like an open door when you're away from the vehicle.

If you're really serious about security, you can even get a system with fingerprint and facial recognition so only certain people can get in, providing ultimate protection for your RV and its contents.

Smart Home Monitoring

For a slightly higher budget than your typical remote camera system, you can invest in a smart remote monitoring system for your RV, which will take into account everything from internal temperature and plumbing status to intrusions and equipment failures, sending a message to your mobile devices if there's any occurring out of the ordinary.

These systems require professional installation, but give you peace of mind knowing that if anything happens to your RV, you'll receive a notification on all of your devices.

Auto Alarm Systems

For a more budget-conscious security system that focuses mostly on deterring intruders, classic vehicle alarm systems will sound an alarm if it detects unauthorized access, and motion detector alarms will sound an alarm and start recording once it detects motion to deter potential thieves.

Steering Wheel and Wheel Clamps

Passive systems that don't require any power sources are a common type of security in RVs. One of these is a steering wheel lock that keeps your RV from being driven away, even if the keys are inside. Some of these locks simply make the steering wheel difficult to turn, while others attach to the brake pedal, making the vehicle impossible to operate until unlocked. It's a simple but effective deterrent.

A comparable system involves attaching locks to your RV's wheels, similar to parking clamps which need to be removed manually before they can be turned.

GPS Trackers and Other Deterrents

There are anti-theft systems available with GPS tracking and the ability to alert authorities once it detects the vehicle has been stolen.

While this would certainly provide peace of mind for the expense, you can also go the more affordable route of affixing a sticker somewhere visible on your RV's windows, informing any potential thieves that your rig is outfitted with such a device.

These stickers are available on Amazon and other places and can be customized to look more authentic.

Staying Healthy on the Road

There's nothing worse than getting sick or injured while you're traveling, so it's important to take care of yourself and your RV to make sure that you feel as well as possible at all times.

Stay Hydrated

One of the most important things to keep in mind when you're out on the road is that you need to stay hydrated. Drinking plenty of water is always a good idea.

Wash Your Hands

In addition to staying hydrated, it's always important to wash your hands whenever you can.

RV Living is much closer to being an outdoor lifestyle than most forms of sticks-and-bricks living. It's a lifestyle that can be incredibly healthy and safe, so all of the usual good habits like regular hand washing will definitely help. While this may seem like common sense to most, it's a good idea to incorporate it into your everyday schedule (especially before and after meals).

One of the primary benefits that hand washing provides is the prevention and the spread of germs and bacteria.

Keeping your RV clean, as discussed in previous chapters, will also work towards this effect. Speaking of which:

Practice Good Kitchen Hygiene

When you're cooking in your RV, it's a good idea to take the same precautions you would in any kitchen. Cleaning as you go, and keeping raw meats separate from other foods will help keep you (and your family) healthy—no matter how small the area you're working in may be.

Protect Yourself from the Sun

Even if you don't plan on spending a ton of time outdoors, you should still wear high SPF sunscreen whenever you are exposed to the sun for an extended period.

Although traveling in an RV does offer a certain amount of protection (since you're not out in the sun with no protection like when you're driving your car), it doesn't offer 100% protection, and—depending on where you're traveling—you may need to apply sunscreen more than once per day.

And, finally:

Get Some Rest

If you're going to be spending a lot of time on the road, you're going to need to get some rest—for you and for your RV.

Chapter Summary

These are some of the most important things to keep in mind when it comes to staying safe and healthy while RVing:

- Specialized RV insurance is available from most major providers and offers much better coverage for RV-specific purposes than general auto insurance.
- Common RV safety mistakes include driving while tired, driving in hazardous weather, not minding the high clearance of your vehicle. You can avoid that last mistake by knowing the height of your RV—including any attachments—and avoiding routes with low clearances.
- Use RV-specific GPS and mobile apps which convey crucial information.
- Necessary safety precautions for your vehicle: always keep your doors locked, invest in a home security system that you can monitor remotely, invest in a vehicle security system, and consider other anti-theft measures such as a device that initiates GPS tracking and alerts the authorities if your vehicle gets stolen.
- Important safety precautions for yourself: Stay rested, stay hydrated, and don't forget sunscreen if needed

FINAL THOUGHTS
YOU'RE WELL ON YOUR WAY

Congratulations!

Not only have you made the important first step of picking up this book on the basics of RV living, but you've made it to the end as well.

Now that you've reached this point, you've already taken the first steps towards a rich and rewarding life as an RV owner and traveler.

While reading this book will give you a good idea of what to expect in the future, there's really no way to know exactly what's going to happen until it does.

What's most important is that you embrace this new lifestyle, take every day as it comes, and enjoy yourself along the way.

A SHORT MESSAGE FROM THE AUTHOR

Hi, I hope you enjoyed the book? I'd love to hear your thoughts!

Many readers do not know how hard reviews are to come by, and how much they help an author.

I would be incredibly grateful if you could take just 60 seconds to write a brief review on Amazon, even if it's just a few sentences!

Thank you for taking the time to share your thoughts!

Your review will genuinely make a difference for me and help gain exposure for my work.

James

Made in the USA
Middletown, DE
26 July 2021